W9-BHE-886

DUE DATE

Desperate Women

A Woman Looks at the Lord's Prayer

Desperate

*Praying Through
Life's Problems*

Women

MELVA LEA

OLIVER
NELSON

A Division of Thomas Nelson Publishers
Nashville

Published in Nashville, Tennessee, by Oliver-Nelson Books, a division of Thomas Nelson,
Inc., Publishers, and distributed in Canada by Lawson Falle, Ltd., Cambridge, Ontario.

Printed in the United States of America.

Library of Congress Cataloging-in-Publication Data

Lea, Melva.
　　Desperate women / Melva Lea.
　　　　p.　　cm.
　　ISBN 0-8407-9124-0 (hard)
　　　　1. Women—Religious life.　2. Lord's prayer.　3. Lea, Melva.
　I. Title.
BV4527.L43　1991
248.8′43—dc20
　　　　　　　　　　　　　　　　　　　　　　　　　　　　91-23272
　　　　　　　　　　　　　　　　　　　　　　　　　　　　CIP

1 2 3 4 5 6 — 96 95 94 93 92 91

DESPERATE: reckless or violent because of despair
VIOLENT: displaying extreme physical or emotional force

—Webster

The kingdom of heaven suffers violence, and
the violent take it by force.

—Jesus Christ (Matt. 11:12)

Therefore, pray . . .

—Jesus Christ (Matt. 6:9)

To my parents

Toxey & Elva Bryant

Who in times of desperation—both theirs and mine—unflinchingly set their faces to seek the Lord, and their voices to cry out to Him. Thank you for the example, perseverance, and power of your prayers.

Contents

Acknowledgments

The apostle Paul wrote, "I am a debtor."

I, too, am a debtor—to the many wonderful, extraordinary, desperate women whom I've had the privilege of serving the last eleven years at Church on the Rock in Rockwall, Texas. Together, the Holy Spirit has gently taught us to continually "look unto Jesus"—and without the inspiration, encouragement, and testimonies of this multitude of friends, there would have been no well of experience from which to draw.

Thank you to those whose actual stories comprise portions of this book.

Thank you to the rest who helped shape the writer. The anguish of your desperation—may it now be turned to a larger good; and the comfort with which you've been comforted by the Lord—may it spill out through these pages to comfort a host of desperate women.

God richly bless you.

Foreword

This book represents, truthfully, the life of a woman who lives what she teaches. The insights and personal anecdotes stem from someone whose walk is a godly one and whose fruit is manifest in the lives of our three teenagers. Melva, my wife, knows how to pray from crisis to breakthrough. How grateful to God I am to have seen that spiritual authority exercised on my behalf! When you pick up this book and share its pages, you too will find much help for those moments when you sense the desperateness of your situation.

God be with you.

Larry Lea

Introduction

I don't pray because I'm spiritual. I pray because I'm desperate!

Never a day passes without its being obvious to me and to any innocent bystanders that I'm a desperate woman in dire need of divine intervention.

Just when I think that I'm fine and everything's O.K., that today I'm not going to embarrass myself or anyone else—I'm going to be "normal" today!—inevitably I'll do it again! Something crazy, something absurd, that makes others wonder who was irresponsible enough to leave me unattended!

For example, we have recorded in our family annals of "Crazy Mother" stories this choice memory. I pulled up to the school with the car loaded with kids: yours, mine, everybody's. Books and lunches were in the trunk, so I stopped the car, popped the trunk, let out the kids, and then drove off—with the trunk lid bouncing in the air and the kids all jumping up and down in the street, that is, all except those who were standing agape with astonishment.

Of course, this insignificant turn of events never registered with me until I rounded the corner. By then I was light years ahead in my day, mentally checking off everything that had to be done and what I needed from the grocery store. That's when this small voice from the backseat said, "Miss Melva, your trunk is open, and you forgot to let them get their books."

I could have added, "And I nearly forgot *you* as well," but didn't as I pulled up to the elementary school door and let out the last of my charges.

Just then my car phone rang—a necessary gadget so that if I get lost, my children can find me. "Uh, Mom," Jo Anna asked bemused, "did you forget something?"

"Who, me?" I fumed. "Never! I planned the whole thing."

So turning around, driving up the one-way drive at the school the wrong way, and making a U-turn, I came to rest in front of the high-school door where an amused crowd had gathered.

"So what else is new?" I asked Jo Anna resignedly as she, Joy, and company collected their belongings.

"Trunk's down now, Mom," Jo Anna yelled.

"Thanks," I muttered and drove off, choosing to laugh instead of cry.

I could have lived with this incident had it been an isolated one, but unfortunately it was the culmination of a week of similar disasters that began when I drove away from the drive-through at the bank *with* the cylinder used to expedite transactions between car and bank teller. (Can you *imagine*?)

Then lunch rolled around and my ever-hungry sixteen-year-old son suggested an Arby's Roast Beef. So I ordered (just like a normal, sane person), paid my money, and *drove off,* with John slowly sinking down in the seat, moaning, "Oh, Mom! I'm *so* embarrassed!"

Well, if that were not enough, to add insult to injury, the next day I went to my pantry and took out a can of soup. Instead of going over to the electric can opener, I walked to the refrigerator, stuck the unopened can under the automatic ice dispenser, and ice came out all over my hand! (Have you *ever* done anything even vaguely this bizarre?)

What a *demented* week! By Friday I was calling out to God, not routinely, but desperately, "Save me from myself! I am a disaster looking for a place to happen! Help me!"

Later I balefully wailed to my husband, "I think I'm losing my mind!" When he failed to deny this, I knew that I was in trouble.

Daffiness may not seem to you a particularly traumatic BIG DEAL unless you are a woman plagued by similar tendencies. In my case I'm not usually given to such bizarre behavior—at least not so consistently!

But during this period of struggle when I desperately clung to God and cried out to Him for direction, I began to come across other women who were desperate. The women had problems that were not at all entertaining, that elicited tears instead of laughter, tremors instead of sighs. Perhaps some of their dilemmas, like mine, could be solved with reduced stress, diet, vitamins, and exercise. But most couldn't. Most were in life-and-death struggles for survival, many of them in a situation similar to that of my friend Gretchen.* The hopes she most cherished—"to be loved, to have my husband as my best friend, and to know he would always be there"—were crushed when he filed for divorce and shortly thereafter remarried.

Gretchen shared, "It was the most devastating time in my life. Never had I experienced so much pain at once. I was totally exhausted emotionally. I felt so fragile inside. Yet the trauma didn't end just because the divorce was final. I have three teenage children, and my work skills were limited. There were so many obstacles to overcome. I felt so scared. I knew without a sovereign move of God in my life, I wouldn't make it."

Mercifully, Gretchen had learned to pray. She had a history with God, years of evidence of His faithfulness and steadfast love. When her mother and father had forsaken her, the Lord had taken her up. Through years of rejection in a loveless marriage, the Lord had become her comfort and lover of her soul. When she needed a car and the rent was due, He provided. During years of mental abuse, He was her peace. When she didn't think she could live another day with her circumstances, His grace really *was* sufficient.

As she told me later, "I desperately hung on to God with everything I had in me. He was my LIFELINE."

And what about *you?* Have you lived long enough to have a "dark night of the soul"? Why did you buy this book? Are you now in a time when you are so far down that you have to look up to see the bottom?

In your desperation do you know that God really, *really* loves *you* and wants to help you?

Do you know how to contact Him?

Are you afraid He won't answer you? Perhaps you've been too bad, or maybe your problem isn't big enough for Him to worry with?

Whatever your question, God anticipated that you would ask it; whatever your problem, He has the answer. You did not catch Him off guard; He is not surprised or appalled—just waiting for you to turn to Him.

Twelve years ago, during a period of soul-searching, gut-wrenching transition (transition can be the pits!), my husband, Larry Lea, began crying out to God to teach him to pray. The result of that

---

*Her name and others throughout the book have been changed to protect their privacy and that of their children.

hard season in our lives was revelation concerning the Lord's Prayer, the prayer Jesus taught His disciples to pray *that covers every need of the human experience.*

Jesus never conducted the seminar "Forty Ways to Heal the Sick" or "Ten Unique Ways to Cast Out Devils." He never instructed eager young preachers on the three-point outline with life applications or offered the course Church Planting 101.

But He left *specific* instructions on how to pray—*twice* in fact (see Matt. 6; Luke 11)—probably because He knew we'd just memorize it and file it, never recognizing its innate power.

But Jesus said in Luke 11:2, "When you pray, say. . . ." He gave a specific outline or guide to aid us in our praying—knowing that whatever our desperation, it would fall under the heading of one of the lines in the prayer.

I do not pretend—even slightly—to be an expert on prayer. JESUS ALONE IS THE EXPERT.

I am just a desperate woman seeking answers to my particular set of life's questions.

I liken myself to the starving beggar who inadvertently stumbled upon an unlocked warehouse full of bread. While stuffing his mouth, coat, and pockets with everything he could lay his hands on, he was suddenly filled with shame. "Why am I keeping this to myself? I must tell my friends!"

So, friend, as one desperate woman beggar to another, may I share with you the bread I have found? Perhaps the Spirit of God can use some of the insights I've gained over the years of living with Larry, a man of prayer, coupled with the wisdom and example of past and present generations of recognized men and women of prayer—put into the outline of the Lord's Prayer—to inspire, guide, or deliver you during your times of desperation.

Whatever your current season of life—trouble or a blessed space of reprieve—above all, I pray this book will ignite your very soul with holy desire to say with the apostle Paul, "That I may know *Him.*"

God bless you.

Your colaborer in Christ,
Melva Lea
Rockwall, Texas

1 It's Always Something!

Admittance to the School of Prayer is by an entrance test with only two questions. The first one is: Are you in real need? The second is: Do you admit that you are helpless to handle that need?

—*Catherine Marshall*

Someone once said, "You know you are in a *real* trial when there is no back door." No resources, no options left, no way of escape short of a miracle. Yes, THIS IS THE BIG ONE!

In times like these, women—even unbelieving ones—find themselves breathing words like, "Oh, God!" and sending short, desperate, heartrending cries heavenward, hoping, praying, that Someone somewhere is bigger and stronger than the situation and will HELP THEM!

Never before in the history of our society has a woman had so many options or so many responsibilities and temptations available to her. She can pursue a corporate career or elect to stay at home. She can become a mother as a result of natural childbirth, adoption, artificial insemination, or a surrogate situation. She can choose husbands and lovers, either/or, both/and, with a minimum of societal criticism and yet at the same time hire a psychoanalyst in hopes of erasing the guilt and work a second shift to pay medical bills arising from the fallacies of "safe sex."

She lives with the knowledge that should she marry, the odds are against her marriage making it. Half of all first marriages now end in divorce, and six out of ten second marriages run extreme possibilities of collapse. She could end up a single parent, the sole support of her children, either through death or divorce, and know the heartbreak of poverty, especially if she is black or Hispanic. Chances are that sometime in her life she will become the caretaker of elderly relatives, whether out of love or necessity or both; and because of lengthened life expectancy, she, too, will be dependent on others.

Knowing that three out of four women will sometime during their lives be sexually assaulted leaves a woman fearful for her life and searching for a serious means of protection. She will buy guard dogs, karate lessons, handguns, and security alarms in addition to dead bolts, ball bats, whistles, and mace.

And then there are the ever-present health problems: PMS; arteriosclerosis; AIDS; arthritis; heart and lung disease; breast, ovarian, and cervical cancer; and others from environmental hazards such as polluted food and water.

In the immortal words of Rosanne Rosanna-Dana, the zany irrepressible character created by the late comedienne Gilda Radner: "It's always something!" Indeed! No wonder women today are desperate! It *is* always something!

One of my favorite authors, Tim Hansel, who lives with debilitating pain resulting from an accident, has written, "We are continually faced by great opportunities brilliantly disguised as insoluble problems."

Jesus said, "In the world you will have tribulation" (John 16:33). This is not a verse that you hang on your refrigerator or mirror to encourage yourself. But it is a fact of life. If you are *living,* you will have problems. Then Jesus added, "But be of good cheer, I have overcome the world."

Now what does that mean? How does this statement move from the realm of "spirituality" and theology into the everyday realm of your life?

When Jesus said that He had overcome the world, He meant that soon He would be the risen Lord; He would be the One who would hold the keys to hell and death; He was the Lamb who would be slain for your sins; He would be beaten for your peace of mind and healing of your body. So when problems occur in our daily lives—tragic or simple—He has already taken the "force of the impact" in His own body. Subsequently He can carry us and cover us and grace us to go right through the middle of the trial with victory in our hearts.

I love Tim Shepherd's song, "He Will Carry You." The picture in it is one found in the Old Testament when the children of Israel forsook the Lord and turned to idol worship. They had gods that could not see or hear, that had hearts of stone, and that had to be *transported on the shoulders of the owners*. In great contrast, God said, "I am not like them in any way. I WILL CARRY *YOU!*"

My precious friend and neighbor Johnnie Willis has lived a lifetime of desperation, but she has chosen to make it work for her good, to make it serve the purposes of God in her life. During these times she has chosen to totally cast herself upon the mercy of God and trust in His love for her. Her life reads something like a history book entitled *All the Wars Since Cain and Abel 'Til Now*. She has survived one battle after another and is one of the most remarkable women I've ever known. She'll be the *first* to admit it's not her own strength or goodness; it has been the goodness of God all the way. Here's how her story reads:

> abused child
> substance abuser
> abusive marriage to professional gambler and drug user
> INTRODUCED TO JESUS!
> heart attack
> miscarriage
> partial hysterectomy
> divorce after thirteen years of marriage
> remarried to a WONDERFUL MAN!
> second miscarriage
> stroke
> third miscarriage (twins)
> tumor on uterus
> lumps in breast
> seizures
> brain tumor

The remarkable thing about Johnnie is that the more awful life treats her, the better she becomes. She looks more like Jesus every day.

I remember when we all prayed that she could carry the twins to term—and she miscarried. All she said was, "God promised to 'perfect that which concerns me,' and He will."

Then she got the growth on her uterus, and the doctors insisted on a hysterectomy. Johnnie said no—she needed that uterus!—she had not yet had a baby, and she believed that she was going to have one. "God will perfect that which concerns me," she stated simply. After

3

prescribed treatment at M. D. Anderson, Houston, and Presbyterian Hospital, Dallas, and much prayer, the tumor disappeared.

But then came that terrible, horrible day when Michael arrived home and found Johnnie unconscious in the middle of a seizure. Diagnosis: brain tumor. It had probably been with her since a child, causing some learning disabilities, and was most certainly responsible for the previous apparent stroke.

Immediately she was rushed into surgery to determine if the tumor was malignant. It was benign. But while in recovery, Johnnie once again began to convulse. Back she went into surgery. Then came the worst possible report: her brain was hemorrhaging. Before the first surgery the doctor had warned her husband, Michael, that if any hemorrhaging should occur, it would impair her ability to walk, talk, and assimilate thoughts. She would have no strength in her right hand and would probably not awaken for two days.

Everyone prayed. Her church friends and pastors prayed. Michael went to the chapel. Molly, our mutual friend, got me on the phone, and we prayed. And then it happened.

Four hours later Johnnie awoke. She squeezed Molly's hand with her right one so hard all the alarms in intensive care went off. Then she looked Molly straight in the eye and said as plainly as a Texan can speak English, "I've had it! I've had it with the devil!"

Those were the words of a fighter. Johnnie was back, and boy, was she mad!

Recuperation was stressful; talking was a chore. At times choosing the right word or placing words in correct sequence would bring tears of frustration to her eyes. But one day as Molly was doing Johnnie's nails, Molly began to pray quietly aloud. All of a sudden Johnnie became excited. "I can do that! I can do that!" she exclaimed. As she listened to Molly, she, too, began to pray, haltingly at first, then more confidently.

The day I interviewed her for this story, Johnnie met Molly and me at the door dressed in bright red walking shorts and a white T-shirt with "JESUS" emblazoned in block letters across her chest. Her beautiful intense blue eyes twinkled beneath the brim of a bright red cap.

"Look at this," she said proudly whisking off the cap to reveal a shorn crown. "My hair is growing back so well. See, my scars are almost covered." Then she snapped the cap back down on her head and adjusted the red bow on what remained of her long dark ponytail.

"The doctor said the tumor is gone," she declared triumphantly. "The Lord promised He would perfect that which concerns me." She paused, then added softly with a smile, "Now I'm about ready for a baby!"

Just giving a cursory glance at this tall slender lovely lady, a casual observer would never detect signs of the catastrophes of Johnnie's life. They are not evident upon her face. On the contrary, she exudes a joyful optimism and love for life. She now drives her own car and once again keeps Michael's expense account. Occasionally when she is tired, she will struggle to find the right word, which I find *quite* miraculous seeing that I often struggle to find the right paragraph and don't have any medical excuse for my ineptitude.

"Johnnie, how have you continued to keep your faith in God intact during these critical times?" I asked her.

"I've just always looked to Jesus and chosen to laugh instead of cry. Since I became saved, I've wanted to know Him better; He's given me the privilege of knowing Him in suffering. And then I've chosen to believe the words He's told me when I'd pray. He really is perfecting that which concerns me!"

As Molly and I left her that day, Isaiah 43:1–3 came into my heart:

> Fear not, for I have redeemed you;
> I have called you by your name;
> You are mine.
> When you pass through the waters,
>   I will be with you;
> And through the rivers, they shall not
>   overflow you.
> When you walk through the fire, you
>   shall not be burned,
> Nor shall the flame scorch you.
> For I am the LORD your God,
> The Holy One of Israel, your Savior.

All the somethings in life can lead us to desperation and panic, or our desperation can lead us to God.

"The opportunities of life lie in our problems," says Tim Hansel. "However hopeless they may seem, unsolvable problems offer us a new opportunity to listen to God in brand-new ways."

Don't let the hard times become your tombstone. Instead, let them become your stepping-stone into a real, living relationship with God.

Oh, that the same could be said of you during your times of desperation as Winston Churchill said of the British Empire in the war years: "This was their finest hour."

2 Why Pray?

God does nothing but in answer to prayer.

—John Wesley

God must help man by prayer. He who does not pray, therefore robs himself of God's help and places God where He cannot help man.

—E. M. Bounds

A very agitated mother flung open the door to admit Larry. "Our son has run away from home," she sobbed as she haltingly recounted the circumstances of the past few hours.

"Thank you for coming, Pastor," her husband managed to say between her sobs. He, too, was having a difficult time. Despair etched his eyes, and his hands trembled as he ran them through his hair.

"We don't know where he is," his wife interrupted, wringing her hands. "We don't know who he's with, if he's safe, or *anything!* What are we going to do?"

"We are not going to worry about it," Larry replied calmly.

The poor woman was so caught off guard that she fairly shouted at him, "Well, if we're not going to worry about it, what *are* we going to do?"

Larry quietly said, "We're going to pray."

Three days later the young man came home.

Reading the old hymns of the church is almost like reading Scripture. This familiar verse by Joseph Scriven is appropriate:

> What a friend we have in Jesus,
> All our sins and griefs to bear!

> What a privilege to carry
> Ev'rything to God in prayer!
> Oh, what peace we often forfeit,
> Oh, what needless pain we bear,
> All because we do not carry
> Ev'rything to God in prayer!

William W. Walford expressed it beautifully when he penned:

> In seasons of distress and grief,
> My soul has often found relief,
> And oft escaped the tempter's snares
> By thy return, sweet hour of prayer.

"Nothing is more important to God than prayer in dealing with mankind," writes E. M. Bounds. It is prayer that moves the hand of God. God does not impose His will upon His creation, although He most assuredly does have a divine will, plan, and purpose for everything He has made.

Our pastor and dear friend, Bob Willhite has been a man of prayer for over forty years. In his enlightening book *Why Pray?* Pastor Willhite says, "God must wait until He is asked before He can do what He wants to do—not because He is powerless, but because of the way He has chosen to exercise His will."

You see, God has put laws into effect that govern all of the created order. You have firsthand knowledge of one of those laws every time an egg rolls off the kitchen counter to make a mess all over your already dirty floor, or when you think, *What's this I feel hanging around my knees?* and realize it's the slip with the old elastic that you should have thrown away before today!

God has limited Himself to work within His own laws and can supersede them only because of the prayers of the saints. To illustrate, let me tell you a story that happened to us years ago in a little church on the plains of west Texas. Out there, nature can throw a fit with alarming violence in an unsuspectingly short time. One evening as Larry was preaching, a heavy rain commenced. When the rain ceased and the wind began to blow violently, one of the ushers suddenly rushed to the front shouting, "A tornado is headed this way!" The congregation jumped up and ran to look outside. Sure enough, already on the ground and moving their way was a large black funnel. Immediately, the people dropped to their knees and began crying out to God. Larry began to lead them in a prayer of agreement: "Lord, we believe You have all power—that You didn't bring us here tonight for our destruction but for Your praise and glory. We ask You to deliver us from this tornado. We command it in the name of Jesus to turn and disappear." At that very moment the funnel, which by now was very close, suddenly stopped its advance, turned, and disappeared back up into the clouds!

The prayers of the saints had allowed God to intervene and *supersede* His own laws of nature.

Willhite says, "The law of prayer is the highest law of the universe—it can overcome the other laws by sanctioning God's intervention. When implemented properly the law of prayer permits God to exercise His sovereignty in a world under the dominion of a rebel with a free will, in the universe governed by natural law."

Johnny Casto was a young rebel exercising his free will without any knowledge of God. All he knew was that tomorrow he would be shipped out to Vietnam, and tonight he was going to have a date with a pretty girl named Kathy. What he didn't bargain for was that Kathy was a real Christian—the kind who believed the Bible. During the course of the evening Kathy shared Jesus with Johnny and told him that she would pray for him every day while he was gone.

True to her word, Kathy began to come into agreement with God every day on Johnny's behalf. She reminded the Lord daily of His promises, that it was not His will that any should perish but all (including Johnny) come to repentance. She declared over him that the eyes of his understanding be enlightened and that he would know the hope of his calling in Jesus; that the god of this world would be bound from blinding his eyes to the truth of the gospel; and that Johnny would receive revelation of the lordship of Jesus.

Johnny had been in Vietnam six weeks when his sergeant, who was directly in front of him, stepped on a land mine. He was killed instantly, and Johnny was severely wounded. As he lay bleeding to death, he began to pray, "God, if You'll have mercy on me, I'll give You my life." It was not just one of those fire escape prayers of the scared or dying. God knew Johnny really meant it. Miraculously, he survived. When he arrived home, he professed his faith in Jesus publicly and asked Kathy to marry him—two great choices! Today, Johnny and Kathy are in full-time ministry preaching and teaching the message of prayer.

By natural law, Johnny should have died. He took the full force of the explosion, his body riddled with shrapnel. But because a little teenage girl was crying out on his behalf, God was enabled by prayer to supersede His own laws and thwart the devil's plan.

The great English pray-er R. A. Torrey wrote in his book *How to Pray:*

> Prayer often avails where everything else fails. How utterly all of Monica's efforts and entreaties failed with her son! But, her prayers prevailed with God, and the immoral youth became St. Augustine, the mighty man of God. By prayer, the bitterest enemies of the gospel have become its most valiant defenders, the most wicked the truest sons of God, and the most contemptible women the purest saints. Oh, the power of prayer to reach down, where hope itself seems vain, and lift men and women up into fellowship with and likeness to God! It is simply wonderful! How little we appreciate this marvelous weapon!

The Lord entreats us, "Call to Me, and I will answer you, and show you great and mighty things, which you do not know" (Jer. 33:3). "He is getting ready to work," Torrey concluded, "and now He is listening for the voice of prayer. Will He hear it? Will He hear it from you?"

3 Desperate Women Pray

Whatever things you ask when you pray, believe that you receive them, and you will have them.

—*Mark 11:24*

The effective, fervent prayer of a righteous man avails much.

—*James 5:16*

Desperation is no respecter of persons, and it does not wait for a convenient time to call.

Janice and John Cruse were fertility patients after five years of a childless marriage. When Janice prematurely delivered twins fifteen weeks ahead of her due date, Weston weighed one pound five ounces and was ten and one-half inches long; Neiman weighed one pound nine and one-half ounces and was twelve and one-fourth inches long. John's wedding band slipped over their arms up to their shoulders with room to spare. Their skin was transparent; every vein could be seen. Their arms and legs looked like pencils. Monitoring wires and catheters ran from every orifice.

Just a few short years earlier, doctors did not even attempt to save babies that weighed less than 700 grams. But because of breakthroughs in prenatal research, Neiman and Weston Cruse were given a chance for survival.

When Janice had become pregnant, she and John were overjoyed. Coming from large, close-knit families, the couple had earnestly desired a family of their own. When they learned it was to be a multiple birth, they were overwhelmed.

Now they were heartbroken. Feeling that it was her fault because she was unable to carry the twins to term, Janice sobbed to the boys,

"Mommy's so sorry," as she looked down upon the pitiful naked stick figures who were her sons. While the hospital team battled to stabilize the babies, Janice, walking the tightrope of fear/faith, began to cry out to God. Desperate women pray.

Although their eyes were not yet opened, the babies knew her voice and would turn their heads in the direction of their mother when she talked to them. They would become excited and kick their tiny arms and legs. So Janice realized she could not continue to grieve in their presence without adversely affecting them. That's when the Lord gave her the Scripture, "A merry heart does good, like medicine" (Prov. 17:22).

"At that point, I decided to receive His word to me—to *choose*—no matter how I felt—to rejoice in the Lord and be a blessing to my babies. It was hard, but I did it! I told John," Janice continued, "I will not be denied what is my inheritance from the Lord. *These* are the children I earnestly desired of Him. *They* are the answers to my prayers. I will not give them over to death without a fight." So Janice began to bombard heaven day and night, crying out her desperate desire to God.

In *The Necessity of Prayer,* E. M. Bounds writes,

> There is no successful prayer without consuming desire. Desire is intense, but narrow. It cannot spread itself over a wide area. It wants a few things and wants them badly. It wants them so badly that nothing but God's willingness to answer can bring it ease and contentment.
> It is this singleness of desire, this definite yearning, which counts in praying and drives prayer directly to the core and center of supply.
> Without desire, there is no burden of the soul, no sense of need, no enthusiasm, no vision, no strength, and no glow of faith. There is no strong pressure, no holding onto God with a deathless, despairing grasp.

Janice embodied such a prayer. Her desire was focused upon the lives of her babies. She held onto God with that "deathless, despairing grasp."

As the weeks passed, much intercession was made on behalf of the children. Each Sunday the latest report was disclosed at church, and the whole church cried out to God on their behalf. Home prayer meetings and ladies' groups, the church prayer chain, and individuals who had heard their stories interceded daily for the boys. Complete strangers would approach Janice on the sidewalk or in the grocery store and say, "The Lord awakened me in the middle of the night to pray for your babies." The prayer response was overwhelming.

During this time, a friend of Janice had a vision while praying. She saw a dark, suffocating cloud hovering over the babies' beds in ICU. Immediately above the children, between them and the cloud, was a bright golden glow. As she prayed, the glow increased; when she ceased, the glow diminished. Again, as she renewed her intensity in prayer, the glow brightened; when she stopped, it waned. The dark cloud she perceived to represent death; the golden glow, the prayers of the saints. This revelation came at just the right moment, for the boys began to digress. For six weeks, they had held their own, but suddenly they were attacked by a virus (CMV). Since they did not yet have natural antibodies, the virus began to rapidly take them down.

The chief doctor, a Christian, on the team working with the babies called John and Janice in to give them the "death talk," to prepare them for the worst. With tears in his eyes he said, "They've done so well for six weeks. I can't believe they're going to die now."

Neiman was particularly critical. His kidneys had not functioned in over forty-eight hours. He was so swollen, he could not open his eyes. The word was sent out that death was imminent unless God intervened. Remembering the vision of the golden glow, the whole household of faith surrounding the Cruses renewed their prayer intensity.

John and Janice encouraged themselves in the Lord with the word that Donny James, a Dallas policeman and member of the church, had given them. "God awoke me in the night with a word for you," he said. "It's the same one He gave me a few years back when our twin girls were born under the same circumstances. Psalm 118:17. They 'shall not die, but live, and declare the works of the LORD.'"

That was the exact word a lady in church had given them that same week!

John and Janice decided to set their hearts on the word of the Lord and waited to see the results.

Later that morning an ecstatic nurse called the anxious couple: "The strangest thing just happened. I just noticed that the prayer cloth pinned onto Neiman's bed was gone. It must have gotten thrown out when the bed was changed. So I cut the one on Weston's bed in two. The minute I pinned the other half onto Neiman's sheet, he began to urinate!" She paused a moment to catch her breath and then added dramatically, "It was spooky!" Both boys rallied, and the church rejoiced.

Neiman and Weston Cruse were hospitalized for five and one-half months. They have had ten operations between them. Today, they are active, inquisitive, *humorous* two-and-a-half-year-olds, both doing well, except that Weston has no growth platelet in one hip. Janice stands firm in faith, however, and says, "How can I doubt that God will take care of this, too, after all the succession of miracles He has done for my sons?"

Alexa is now ten months old—the final addition to the Cruses' desire for a family. She was born with a hole in her heart (which has since totally disappeared through prayer). She weighs more than either of the boys!

I went to see Janice the other day. Alexa was asleep for a while, looking like a blonde pink-cheeked cherub. Neiman was talking a blue streak, and Weston was busy undressing himself, preferring to be au naturel.

It's as though this couple who were determined to see their "desire accomplished" and have a family of their own now have triplets. I asked Janice how she managed to keep her faith—and sanity—with the events of the last three years. She replied simply with a sweet smile, "I moved out—and *He* moved in."

Another desperate woman I have loved since childhood was the object of ridicule by her husband's second wife because she was barren. How deeply she longed for a son! So Hannah chose the only way out of her suffering and the bitter relationship—she prayed.

First Samuel records, "And she was in bitterness of soul, and prayed to the LORD and wept in anguish. . . . Now Hannah spoke in her heart; only her lips moved, but her voice was not heard" (1:10, 13). Hannah prayed silently but *fervently,* and God heard her prayer. He avenged her of her adversary by opening her womb and giving her a son, Samuel, the great prophet and judge of Israel, whom she dedicated to the Lord. She said, "For this child I prayed, and the LORD has granted me my petition which I asked of Him" (1:27). Then the Lord blessed her abundantly above all she could ask or think by giving her three more sons and two daughters.

Pastor Bob Willhite says,

> We must pray with emotion to be heard. Jesus prayed—aloud and with emotions. Hebrews 5:7 says of Jesus: "Who, in the days of His

flesh, . . . offered up prayers and supplications, with vehement cries and tears to Him who was able to save Him from death, and was heard. . . ." The Word of God assures us that our high priest can be "touched with the feeling of our weaknesses" (Hebrews 4:15, KJV). Feelings—emotions—do touch our Lord.

Emotions are a vital part of prayer. . . . As James 5:16 says, "The effectual fervent prayer of a person in right standing with God releases tremendous power" (Willhite's paraphrase). Effectual prayer is fervent. The greater the need, the more intensely we feel it.

To me, it would not be emotionally or psychologically honest to come before God with a religious prayer. (O Thou most high God, Creator of heaven and earth, hear the plea of this Thy humble servant as I calmly communicate with Thee about this emergency.) To be honest, we should lift up our voices with strong crying and tears.

I remember a time years ago when I happened to glance in on my then ten-year-old daughter, Jo Anna. She was lying upon her bed, face to the wall, sobbing her heart out to God. Rascal, her beloved tomcat whom she had rescued from starvation and abandonment when only a kitten, was in the final stages of feline leukemia. That afternoon in the vet's office, Dr. Archie had looked at Rascal and said with regret in his voice, "There's nothing I can do. Would you like for me to put him to sleep? He's only got a few hours left." Unwilling to shock Jo Anna by returning empty-handed, I declined and took Rascal home to tell the family the sad news.

But Jo Anna was not willing to give up so easily. She had just completed a summer project of reading through the entire Bible, and her faith was high. She had seen how again and again God had mercy on His people and answered their prayers. Now as I glanced in on her, she reminded me of the story of King Hezekiah (see 2 Kings 20). The king had become very ill, and the prophet Isaiah told him to put his house in order, for God said he would die. But Hezekiah turned his face to the wall and cried out to God. God granted him fifteen more years of life. So likewise, here was Jo Anna, face to the wall, pouring out to God the deep longing of her young heart.

We made a bed for the dying emaciated white creature with orange ear and tail in a warm, quiet corner and waited for the inevitable to happen.

But do you know, that cat got hungry when I started cooking supper? He came tottering stiffly into the kitchen, begging in a pitiful voice for something to eat. He ate everything I gave him! The next morning he was up, loudly insisting on breakfast. Then he gave himself a bath, stretched, rolled around in a pool of sunshine, and took an arrogant stroll about the yard. We looked at him in amazement. He was a miracle! That cat lived two more years—his old fat, sassy, squirrel-and-bird-chasing self—all because a desperate little lady grabbed hold of God and would not let Him go until He gave her the deepest desire of her heart.

David was a mighty king credited with uniting Israel and subduing all her enemies. He was a man of violence, a great warrior. He was no less when he stood before God with the desperate needs of his heart. He did not pray anemic, religious prayers. On the contrary, he prayed with great intensity and desire, pouring out his very soul to God. In Psalm 69 he cried,

> Save me, O God!
> For the waters have come up to my neck.
> I sink in deep mire,
> Where there is no standing;
> I have come into deep waters,
> Where the floods overflow me.
> I am weary with my crying;
> My throat is dry;
> My eyes fail while I wait for my God (vv. 1–3).

On numerous occasions when I did not know how to voice my own cry, King David's words became my own; his cries of desperation and pain, faith and hope, mine. I broke through to God, and He broke through upon me.

I became violent in my pursuit of God, even as Jacob, the Hebrew patriarch of old, when he was wrestling with the angel. Like him, I cried, "I will not let You go unless You bless me"—even as did Janice Cruse, Jo Anna Lea, Hannah, and a multitude of other women through the centuries.

Do you have a God-given desire?

Are you desperate?

Are you willing to direct that desperation toward God in prayer?

If so, His promise to you is this:

The LORD is near to all who call upon Him,
To all who call upon Him in truth.
He will fulfill the desire of those who fear Him;
He also will hear their cry and save them (Ps. 145:18–19).

4 Will God Answer My Prayers?

Beloved, if our heart does not condemn us, we have confidence toward God. And whatever we ask we receive from Him, because we keep His commandments and do those things that are pleasing in His sight.

—1 John 3:21–22

"But will God really answer *my* prayers?" you may ask. "I'm not sure He likes me. Do I know the rules and meet all the requirements? Prayer is a mystery to me. It seems hard."

God loves you. He needs you. He desires to show Himself strong for you. But there are conditions to be met in order for your prayers to be answered.

In this age of instant winners, rapid-film-developing cameras, fast food, and faster divorces, we often expect God to respond in like fashion—instantly. Because God loves us, He will not allow us to treat Him like a puppet on a string or a butler on call. If we give Him the opportunity, He will grow us up to hold Him in His rightful position of reverence and respect, knowing that, yes, He can be touched with our feelings of infirmity. But at the same time, He is not like us; He is greater and also, as the song says, "greater than all our need."

Truly, the Scriptures are full of "great and precious promises," such as these:

Whatever you ask in My name, that I will do, that the Father may be glorified in the Son. If you ask anything in My name, I will do it (John 14:13–14).

Whatever things you ask when you pray, believe that you receive them, and you will have them (Mark 11:24).

If two of you agree on earth concerning anything that they ask, it will be done for them by My Father in heaven (Matt. 18:19).

But when you look at the whole of Scripture, you realize such promises also have conditions.

Bob Willhite says,

God will not do those things for me which are contrary to His loving nature. He will not do anything which would cause Him to violate His holy character. He will do nothing that is wrong. He does not answer the prayers of rebels and the willfully disobedient, unless those prayers are asking for forgiveness. He will not answer those who are selfish and self-centered. God will not do for us what He told us to do, that is, we cannot delegate to God what He delegated to us. Do you see? "Whosoever" does not apply to everyone. "Anything" does not mean "everything."

James speaks straight to this issue: "You ask and do not receive, because you ask amiss, that you may spend it on your pleasures [lusts, KJV]" (4:3).

Yes, there are conditions to God's promises. Let me illustrate.

Suppose I said to Joy, my younger daughter, "Joy, when you go to college, you'll be responsible for your own laundry. So today, in preparation for that time, we are going to study Laundry 101. Gather up all your dirty clothes and take them downstairs."

After explanations about whites and darks, soap and bleach, hot and cold, the mechanics of the washer, dryer, and steam iron, I leave her with this final word: "If you need anything else, just call me and I'll get it for you."

As she works, Joy begins to think about what I said, "If you need anything else, just call me and I'll get it for you."

She thinks, "My mom is honest. I can trust her word. She said anything . . ."

So she calls, "Mom, I need something."

"O.K., sweetheart," I reply. "What is it?"

"A red BMW convertible. I need that for school, too. I don't want to have to walk everywhere."

Now do you think that's what I meant when I said "anything"? Of course not. "Anything" applied only to those things necessary for doing laundry.

Often we are like small children with our list for Santa: "God, I want this and this and this and . . . God, You *promised!*"

And when He fails to respond as we think He should, we stomp off with our feelings hurt, thinking that God doesn't love us or that there is something wrong with our faith or, worse still, that something is wrong with God's Word.

If your two-year-old child demanded to play with the butcher knife, would you give it to him? Or what if your twelve-year-old requested the car for the evening?

Likewise, if God gave us everything we asked Him for, we'd end up with everything we ever wanted but not wanting most of what we got!

Dr. Robert Schuller wrote it this way:

> If the idea is not right—
> God answers
> "No"
>
> If the timing is not right—
> God answers
> "Slow"
>
> When *You* are not right—
> God answers
> "Grow!"
>
> God never answers
> the prayers of people
> until *they* are ready for it.

Sometimes when we are baby believers, God will answer our outrageous prayers immediately—that we might learn to trust Him. But as we get older in Him, He requires more of us. Then John 14:13-14 takes on a broader perspective: "Whatever you ask by *My* command and authority, acting in *My* behalf, for the advancement of *My* kingdom, I will do, that the Father may be glorified in the Son" (Willhite paraphrase). Dr. Schuller observes, "Prayer is not a scheme whereby we can move God to our lives; rather it is a spiritual exercise where we draw ourselves to God until we are part of His plan and His purpose." Matthew 6:33 commands us, "Seek first the *kingdom of God and His righteousness,* and all these things shall be added to you" (emphasis added). In other words, if we'll take care of God's interests, He'll take care of those things that concern us.

But what about the failures in prayer? The road of life is strewn with disillusioned pray-ers, who to the best of their ability met the conditions and yet their prayers were not answered. Many are heartsick; as the Scripture says, "Hope deferred makes the heart sick" (Prov. 13:12).

I'm reminded of one such precious lady I knew years ago. She was a faithful intercessor, a loving wife and mother; she believed the promises of God and tried to walk humbly with the Lord. But one day her husband lost his prestigious job and refused to take lesser employment. Consequently, he went without work for almost three years. In the interim, they lost their house, their car, their life savings. Then as a final blow, her father was diagnosed with cancer. He willingly took the prescribed medical treatments, received the prayers of the saints, believed he would be healed—and died. My friend's faith was severely wounded. It took her many years to trust God again.

It is true. Bad things really do happen to good people.

Even as I am writing this, I am very much aware that we live in a world where all the answers are not available. The apostle Paul said, "For now we see in a mirror, dimly" (1 Cor. 13:12). Within three consecutive weekends in Dallas, three teenage boys were killed; two were in our church, and the other was the son of a prominent minister. Two of the boys were murdered in separate incidents, the third killed in a car wreck involving a drunk driver. None of it makes sense; it appears so futile that they all died in vain. Their deaths were not good. The unfathomable grief of the parents, families, and friends is not a good thing.

In times like these, we must doubt our doubts and choose to believe the Word of God. God did not say all things were good, but He promised to work all things *together* for good to those who love the Lord and are the called according to His purpose (see Rom. 8:28).

This is not a cliché, a "catchall" for someone who cannot face the reality of the moment. On the contrary, it is a great promise of redemption in the midst of tribulation. Jesus said, "Come to Me, all you who labor and are heavy laden, and I will give you rest" (Matt. 11:28). And again the Scripture encourages us, "Cast your burden on the LORD, and He shall sustain you" (Ps. 55:22).

God knows the cruelties and uncertainties of life on this earth. He learned firsthand through the life and death of Jesus. But in all our despair and questions and grief, He says, "Just come to Me; give it all to Me, and I will *make* it work for your good."

I was meditating on this promise one day and was suddenly struck with the overwhelming greatness of God. When the Scripture says *all things,* it's not just referring to the good things. If God worked only good things together for our good, what would be the miracle in that? But He works *all* things together for good—that means *the worst conceivable things.* He'll take all of them and *make* them work for good, for those who love Him and are part of His purpose in the earth. Now, what an awe-inspiring, bigger-than-anything-you-can-imagine God is He?

We are His workmanship—*His* to command—not vice versa.

He is the great Creator, the One who can fix you where you're broken.

Are you willing to come to Him regardless of the depth of your desperation, regardless of the number of your questions? Are you willing to commit your life to Him regardless of the outcome?

> Then shall you call, and the LORD will answer;
> You shall cry, and He will say, "Here I am" (Isa. 58:9).

> > Did is a word of achievement,
> > Won't is a word of retreat,
> > Might is a word of bereavement,
> > Can't is a word of defeat,
> > Ought is a word of duty,
> > Try is a word each hour,
> > Will is a word of beauty,
> > Can is a word of power.
> > —Anonymous

Can is your word, too. You can make your desperation work for your good. You can use it to learn how to pray, and pray effectively. God really does want to answer you.

Jesus has given you the pattern.

The Holy Spirit will give you the grace.

"In this manner, therefore, pray: "Our Father . . .""

5 Desperate to Have a Father

"Our Father . . ."

I will be a Father to you,
And you shall be My sons and daughters,
Says the LORD Almighty.

—*2 Corinthians 6:18*

Jesus' twelve disciples were never accused of being megabrains or too spiritual. Instead, like most of us, it took them a while to catch on to what He was doing. They noticed that He spent a large portion of each day praying and occasionally remembered the great message He had preached a couple of years before while teaching the multitude on the Mount of Beatitudes at which time He had given them a prayer outline.

JUDAS:—"What an admirable leader He is!"

JOHN:—"So spiritual, too!"

ANDREW:—"Can you believe the hours He prays?"

MATTHEW:—"What do you suppose He finds to talk to God about for so long?"

PETER:—"Yeah, I'd run out of things to say!"

JAMES:—"It wears me out to try to keep up with Him. He never sleeps!"

THOMAS:—"I doubt if I could ever pray that way."

At that point in time, prayer was not a priority with the disciples. Prayer was something *Jesus* did. They were just His buddies along for the ride, enjoying the excitement and adventure that surrounded them when they were with Jesus.

But they began to notice that there really might be something to the prayer thing. *Jesus went from one place of prayer to the next and in between did miracles.* He would pray and then heal the sick; He would pray, and demons would flee; He would pray—and raise the dead?!

Wow! That was great!

What was *not* so great was when Jesus was not available and people brought their needs to the Twelve. The crowds of people expected them to do miracles just like Jesus. After all, they were His disciples, weren't they? Humiliated when their futile attempts failed, they remembered His words: "This kind can come out by nothing but *prayer* and fasting" (Mark 9:29, emphasis added).

Prayer! Maybe now was the time to learn to pray!

Together the disciples went to find Jesus. Interrupting His quiet time, one of His disciples, perhaps Andrew who had previously been a disciple of John the Baptist, said to Him, "Lord, teach us to pray, as John also taught his disciples" (Luke 11:1). This time they listened as though they each had four ears.

Jesus said to them, "When you pray, say: Our Father . . ."

The foundation for the remainder of the prayer flows out of the address, "Our *Father*."

When we pray, we are not chanting monosyllables to the ceiling or talking by long-distance to some disinterested deity way out there somewhere. We are talking to our heavenly Father, the One of whom it is recorded in John 3:16: "God [our Father] so loved the world [*you*] that He gave [it cost Him] His only begotten Son [Jesus]."

It has been said that the difference between other world religions and Christianity is that all other religions are man's attempt to reach God, but Christianity is God's attempt to reach man. He initiated the action because He loves *you*.

The name *Father* should be our absolute bottom line, our solid rock on which to lay the foundation of our otherwise shaky, crumbling, or tempestuous life experiences. Unfortunately, we live in such a devil-perverted society and age, the term *Father* conjures up a host of phantoms so that instead of running *to* our Father, we run *from* Him. As Floyd McClung, Jr., wrote in his book *The Father Heart of God,*

> Our world is plagued by an epidemic of pain. With divorce rampant and child abuse screaming from the national headlines, it is

not surprising that for many people the concept of a *Father* God evokes responses of anger, resentment and rejection. Because they have not known a kind, caring earthly father, they have a distorted view of the heavenly Father's love.

One young man said, "If God's anything like my old man, you can have Him." The "old man" had raped the boy's sister repeatedly and regularly beaten his mother.

Perhaps you have never thought of yourself as desperate for a Father. You may think, *I've already got a pretty good one. I don't need another.* Or your reaction may be, *I've already had to put up with one—I don't* want *another.* Or maybe, *I never had a father,* and you yearn for the perfect fantasy one that you've pieced together from admirable characteristics of men you have read about or seen.

But regardless of past experiences, each person on this planet has a basic desperate need for a Father, a warm, loving, understanding, patient, securing, strong, able Father.

Our Father made us that way. And only He is big enough to fill that order.

Reba's understanding of God as Father came through her dad, a lieutenant in the air force, a Captain von Trapp sort (remember the movie *The Sound of Music*?). Although he didn't blow a whistle like the captain, Reba's dad did run his home much like a military installation. Upon his return home from duty, family inspection was the first order of the day, and woe be unto anyone who did not measure up to his expectations. When she was seventeen Reba was grounded for one month because she was five minutes late from a date. (It didn't impress her father that she had been on the front porch the whole time. She was not in the *house*!) Not until she was twenty years old did her father ever tell her that he loved her. When Reba became a Christian, she had difficulty relating to God as her Father. What was He like? Was He unnecessarily harsh and strict? Would He ever take her feelings into account? Did He really love *her* or just her performance? She could relate to Jesus as Savior and Lord but God as *Father?*

What about Elizabeth, whose alcoholic father could never give her himself, so he gave her things? How could she relate to "Father" God when her memories of her earthly father were filled with anger, bitterness, distrust, and rejection?

How can a woman understand God as Father and realize her need of Him when her father and other male authority figures in her life have only taken advantage of her? How can she see God as loving if she was a sexually exploited child or a battered woman?

My daddy is eighty-three years old. Throughout my life he has always been a man of integrity whose word has been his bond. His philosophy of life has always been simple: trust God, and treat others the way you want to be treated. On Saturday night while Mama studied, preparing to teach her Sunday school class the next morning, Daddy and I would watch "Gunsmoke" together. Then he'd read the jokes in *Reader's Digest* while I attempted a manicure on the nubs I called fingernails. Now this was not just *some* Saturday nights but *every* Saturday night. In our home, life was totally predictable. (That changed, never to be the same when I married Larry Lea!)

Daddy has a great sense of humor, and he would sit there reading the jokes to me, chuckling, turning red in the face, and finally getting so tickled that Mama would call us down and close the door because we were too loud.

Because of my God image as modeled to me by Daddy, God was Someone who was faithful, steady, trustworthy, and had a sense of humor; Someone with whom I could be comfortable; Someone who enjoyed my presence as much as I did His.

But as wonderful as my daddy is, he is only human. He cannot fill the void designed for my heavenly Father alone to fill.

"Translating the image of God the Father into human terms is difficult," writes Lois Mowday in *Daughters Without Dads*. "A man living up to that image is as rare and as wonderful as a woman living up to the image of the wife in Proverbs 31." She continues, "We must realize that no earthly man can fulfill the model given us by God the Father, and we must acknowledge that human fathers will fail in many ways."

We still have the God-given basic need for a Father who is bigger than life and stronger than death, who always has the answer and the power to make it happen. We desperately need to know *God* as our Father.

But we have denigrated and limited God in our lives by relegating the treatment we have received at the hands of our earthly fathers to Him. We have given Him a persona that is not His.

God said, "You thought that I was altogether like you" (Ps. 50:21). A. W. Tozer said it well, "We must break the habit of thinking of the Creator as we think of His creatures."

He is not like us.

What Is God Like?

"With the progress of man's intellectual apprehension of the greatness of the universe," asserts G. Campbell Morgan, the great Bible expositor,

> there has been an increase necessarily in his conception of the God of the universe, until at last God has grown out of knowledge and men have declared that He is unknowable, and have defined Him as force, as intelligence—or as the operation of force and intelligence combined. The greater the universe, the greater the God, and the greater the God, the less man has been able to appreciate his relation to Him.

God is infinitely great but nonetheless intimately involved with His own. Charles Haddon Spurgeon said, "He who counts the stars and calls them by their names, is in no danger of forgetting His own children. He knows [you] as thoroughly as if you were the only creature He ever made, or the only saint He ever loved."

What is God like? Philip, one of the twelve disciples, also asked that question. "Lord," he said, "show us the Father, and it is sufficient for us."

Jesus answered, "Have I been with you so long, and yet you have not known Me, Philip? He who has seen Me has seen the Father; so how can you say, 'Show us the Father'?" (John 14:8–9).

G. Campbell Morgan writes in *The Westminster Pulpit,*

> Then Philip saw the meaning of the things he had seen and had never seen, the things he had looked upon and had never understood. Then Philip found that having seen Jesus he had actually seen the Father. . . . When he looked upon One Who embodied in His own personality all the facts of the law and righteousness, he had seen God. . . . When he had looked upon One Who could touch the loaves of a lad until they fed a multitude, and One Who could deal with the spiritual needs of restless hearts until they were rested, he had seen God. . . . When he had seen a Man Who shrank from sorrow yet pressed into it because through it in co-operation with God He could ransom humanity, he had seen God.

He had seen "the image of the invisible God" in whom "dwells all the fullness of the Godhead bodily" (Col. 1:15; 2:9).

He had seen love. Love that is not based upon performance. Unconditional love. The very essence of God, His very nature. Love that illustrates supremely that if the child should wander away, the Father will suffer everything to save and bring it home again. "God is the Father Who will sacrifice Himself to save the child," adds Morgan.

"God is love. God's heart hungers after love. God can only be satisfied with love," continues Morgan.

> Listen to the wailing minor threnody of the old Hebrew prophets. They are from beginning to end the sighing of God after the love of His people. . . . I had thought of them as men of wrath, uttering denunciation of sin and proclaiming the terrible judgment of God's holiness. They are all that; but I found that at the back of all the thunder was the infinite disappointment of God because men did not love Him. "How shall I give thee up, Ephraim?" That is the cry of a Being hungry for love. If you go a little further back in your Bible to the old story in Genesis, you find God saying to Adam, "Where art thou?" That is not the arresting voice of a policeman. It is the wailing voice of the Father Who has lost His child. God is hungry for love.

Love is the all-encompassing characteristic of His nature. Joy, peace, longsuffering, kindness, goodness, faithfulness, humility, and self-control (see Gal. 5:22–23) are the multifaceted expressions of that love. But to understand the ultimate expression of the Father's love, listen to the words of Romans 5:8: "But God demonstrates His own love toward us, in that while we were still sinners, Christ died for us."

Oh, the height and depth, length and breadth of the love of God! "While we were still sinners," while we were enemies of God, the Father "gave His only begotten Son, that whoever believes in Him should not perish but have everlasting life" (John 3:16).

Should we not then receive with full thankfulness of heart the Father's love and return ours to Him? To this A. W. Tozer replies, "Being who He is, God is to be loved for His own sake. . . . Beyond this the angels cannot think."

You Are Adopted

Contrary to popular opinion, we are not all children of God. Jesus said to the Pharisees, "You are of your father, the devil" (John 8:44). That's a pretty arresting statement. John 1:12–13 specifically defines who are children of God: "*But as many as received Him* [Jesus], *to them He gave the right to become children of God, even to those who believe in His name:* who were born not of blood, nor of the will of the flesh, nor of the will of man, but of God" (emphasis added).

June Hunt wrote in her daily devotional, *Seeing Yourself Through God's Eyes,* "Even though God already had a Son, He chose to adopt you. God did not *have* to adopt you; He *wanted* you! You are His child. . . . He is your loving Father."

"For you did not receive the spirit of bondage again to fear," the apostle Paul wrote to his friends in Rome. "But you received the Spirit of adoption by whom we cry out, 'Abba, Father'" (Rom. 8:15). Do not draw back through fear; instead cry, "Father!"

Do not take offense that you are adopted. God already had an "only begotten Son" long before you and I came along. But He saw our great need. We were fatherless, unprotected, under the bondage of the devil and fear of death. To the detriment of His own Son, God the Father brought us into His family. He made us joint heirs with Jesus and gave us His name. Now our name is no longer one of sin or degradation, of shame or failure. It is the name of strength and beauty, of wholeness and holiness: "Old things have passed away; behold, all things have become new" (2 Cor. 5:17). We have been brought into God's family.

First John proclaims, "Behold what manner of love the Father has bestowed on us, that we should be called children of God!" (3:1). Because of this great love, the Father has given us an eternal entrance into His presence by the blood of Jesus.

The Blood of Jesus

People who are spiritually honest instinctively know that they are separated from God because of sin. Adam and Eve in the Garden *hid* from God after they had partaken of the forbidden fruit. When we sin, it is natural for us to run *from* God instead of *to* Him because our sinful condition condemns us before Him, a holy God. Consequently, how can we, sinful flesh, approach a holy God with confidence, even if He *is* our Father and we are His children?

When the Israelites were in Egypt, the people were taught that life could be obtained only by the death of a substitute. Life was possible only through *the blood* of a life given in their place. The blood of the sacrificial lamb had to be sprinkled on the doorframe: "When I see the blood I will pass over you." The death angel would pass on by. They would be saved by the blood of the lamb.

For fifteen centuries Israel lived with the Holy One tabernacled in their midst. But they could not enter into the Holy Place upon penalty of death. Their sin separated them from a holy God. Only once a year could the high priest enter His presence—and then only with blood. Without blood there could be no access by sinful man to a holy God.

Then John the Baptist entered the scene and, pointing to Jesus, announced, "Behold! The Lamb of God who takes away the sin of the world!" (John 1:29).

Jesus knew from the beginning who He was—the Lamb of God—and that He had come to earth for one purpose—to shed His blood—that *sinners,* "whosoever will," those who wanted to be children of God, could be cleansed of sin and given access to the Father's presence. When Jesus cried, "It's finished!" thus signifying that redemption's work was done, the veil of the temple was ripped in half from top to bottom. An everlasting entrance had been opened into our Father's presence. Now because of His sacrifice, we have *boldness* to enter the holiest by the blood of the Lamb (see Heb. 10:19–22).

In his book, *Let Us Draw Nigh,* Andrew Murray, the great apostle of prayer at the turn of the twentieth century, wrote,

> *Enter in!* the veil is rent; the Holiest is open. . . . Oh, the blessedness of a life in the Holiest! Here the Father's face is seen and His love tasted. Here the soul, in God's presence, grows to more complete oneness with Christ, and into more entire conformity to His likeness. Here, in union with Christ in His unceasing intercession, we are emboldened to take our place as intercessors, who can have power with God and prevail. Through the blood, our heart can be God's sanctuary.

His blood has made possible your cleansing and adoption into the family of God. You now have immediate access to your Father's throne. What you could not secure for yourself, Jesus did through His blood.

Joyfully and with greater understanding, we can now obey the instruction of the psalmist:

> Enter into His gates with thanksgiving,
> And into His courts with praise.
> Be thankful to Him, and bless His name (Ps. 100:4).

"Oh, will you not this day believe that that blood gives you, sinful and feeble as you are, liberty, confidence, boldness to draw nigh, to enter the very Holiest?" pleads Murray. "Understand how the Father's heart longs that His children draw near to Him boldly. He gave the blood of His Son to secure it. Let us honour God, and honour the blood, by entering the Holiest with great boldness."

Matthew 11:27 declares that no one knows "the Father except the Son, and [she] to whom the Son wills to reveal Him."

Jesus wills to reveal the Father to *you*. As the only begotten Son of God, He alone has the authority to personally escort you past the blood-covered altar and right into the throneroom of God.

Let nothing hinder you. Together with Jesus cry, "Our Father . . . ," and with thanksgiving and praise, boldly ENTER IN!

6 Desperate to Be Immortal

". . . in heaven, . . ."

Let not your heart be troubled. . . . In my Father's house are many
mansions; if it were not so, I would have told you. I go to prepare a
place for you.

—John 14:1–2

The fear of death is the oldest fear known to man. It is feared by the
high and low of both genders, all races, technologically advanced or
undeveloped Third World countries. The fact is, we are all daily reminded and shockingly appalled by the limitations of our mortality—
the feebleness and brevity of this flesh, the backache, the sudden
fender bender, the need for eyeglasses and bridgework and antacids,
the smashed finger.

What is life? A vapor that soon passes away.

Consequently, each of us is desperate to extend life, whether by
"cheating death" or doing some great philanthropic, altruistic act
that shall speak of our "greatness" long after we're gone. We all long
for immortality, desperate to be remembered so that our lives are not
perceived as inconsequential, unappreciated, or unnoticed.

While death was not uppermost in my mind, it was a part of the
reality of my childhood. I learned early that it was part of life.

The father of one of my playmates was the town undertaker. My
friend and her family lived on the second floor of the funeral home.
When I went to her house to play, I entered the family quarters
through the "viewing room," often past an open casket.

I am an only child, and my mother took me everywhere she went.
Our family's life was built around our local church where Daddy was
a deacon and Mama taught Sunday school. Because they genuinely
loved people, Mama and I paid a visit every time anyone was in the

hospital. When the people returned home, we took them an apple pie. If they died, we attended the funeral. Daddy was often a pallbearer. So early on, I made some observations about death.

I learned that *death is not pleasant*. I saw a playmate's puppy get hit by a car and suffer in agony on the sidewalk while neighbors helplessly looked on.

I learned that *death is not just for the old*. I remember standing shyly in a small living room near a rented hospital bed and looking wonderingly at the girl lying upon it while my mama read to her and her grieving parents words of comfort and hope, the promises of heaven. She was twelve years old. She died of leukemia.

As a young teen, I learned *death is not considerate*. One Sunday morning our family awoke to an early phone call: my mother's father had died during the night. While the extended family was still reeling from the shock of his death, the very next Sunday morning a second call came. My mother's eldest brother, too, had passed away during the night. The multiplied trauma was so profound, Mama can't talk about it even now, twenty-five years later, without tears.

As a midteen, I learned *death is not just*. My precious grandmother came to live with us not long after the death of her beloved husband. She exemplified Jesus more than anyone I have ever known. And yet she died within a year of cervical cancer complicated by uremic poisoning and seizures.

As an older teen, I learned even more vividly how *death is never expected*. It is always shocking. Our friends, Fred and Dot, were still newlyweds when Fred started complaining of discomfort in his kidneys. Dot drove him to the hospital where tests were run throughout the day to determine the cause of the pain. That evening as Dot prepared to go home, Fred said to her, "I'll see you in the morning." The next morning when Dot returned, Fred's bed was empty. He was gone. He had died during the night of polycystic kidneys.

Our modern society goes to extremes to ignore and postpone death. Men and women alike search out the latest wrinkle cream or cosmetic surgery to continue looking as young as possible. Our fashions are so carefully designed to obliterate age differences that a forty-year-old (me!) can easily wear the same clothing as her thirteen-year-old daughter (*my* clothes, which unfortunately never seem to stay in *my* closet!), just maybe not with the same effect.

Megavitamins and horrendous concoctions of herbs, roots, leaves, and bark line our kitchen counters and refrigerator shelves. Exercise, aerobic designed to keep the ole heart and lungs operable longer, and weights to make our flab turn into rock-hard muscle like our teenage sons are touted to stave off the aging process. Like Ponce de León, everyone is looking for a fountain of youth. All of these aids, wonderful as they may be, may prolong our lives and affect their quality but cannot deter forever the inevitable. We are all going to die. Someday, somewhere, some way.

What an uncomfortable thought! It speaks too much of the unknown, and that is one of the most disconcerting things about death. It's so *unknown*.

That reminds me of the fears and discomfort of a woman I knew years ago in college whose husband was being transferred to England. She had a very comfortable, well-ordered life here in the States. She had lived in the same small town all her life and knew all her merchants personally. Her children had some of the same teachers who had taught her as a child. Now she was faced with the unknown. Where would she buy groceries? How would she learn to make change in a foreign currency? Would her children adjust to another system of schooling? Who would become their friends? What about a family doctor? How would she ever learn to drive on the "wrong side" of the street? Her discomfort was acute. She became so depressed and overwhelmed by the unknown that she spent many days in bed with the covers pulled over her head. But denial of the fact did not lessen its reality. The movers arrived; she and her family moved to England. But she was unprepared.

Hiding from death will not prepare us for it. Billy Graham said in his wonderful book *Facing Death and the Life After,* "If we are in a battle with this enemy called DEATH, I believe we should learn about it, in order to know how to confront the dying experience."

Each race and every culture that has ever existed on this planet has struggled to better understand this mystery. Today, many different voices speak to us on this subject. It is confusing. How can we know what to believe?

Buddhists and Hindus purport that death is just a part of the reincarnation cycle; that a person will return again to this earth as another being. That's an intriguing thought but not scriptural. God's Word says, "It is appointed for men to die *once,* but after this the judgment" (Heb. 9:27, emphasis added).

Taoists believe death is a wonderful oblivion: no pain, no choices, no consciousness. The end. Fini. First Corinthians 13:12 puts that philosophy into oblivion: "For now we see in a mirror, dimly, but then face to face. Now I know in part, but then I shall know just as I also am known."

Moslems contend that seven heavens replete with carnal pleasure and spiritual bliss await the faithful who sacrifice themselves here on earth in the cause of the jihad. But no matter how noble the cause, works of righteousness will not gain a soul admittance into heaven. Why? Because as Romans 3:23 explains, "For all have sinned and fall short of the glory of God." "We are all like an unclean thing," wrote the prophet Isaiah, "and all our righteousnesses are like filthy rags" (Isa. 64:6). Centuries later, the apostle Paul expanded this thought and revealed the key to eternal life: "For the wages of sin is death, but the gift of God is eternal life *in Christ Jesus our Lord*" (Rom. 6:23, emphasis added).

Judaism teaches that a person can face death and the joys of heaven if the "good" of her life outweighs the "bad." But once again this falls short because it leaves the ability to make heaven on our end of the ladder, and our ladder is not tall enough! Ephesians 2:8–9 announces, "For by *grace* you have been saved through faith, and that not of yourselves; it is the gift of God, *not of works,* lest anyone should boast" (emphasis added).

What about all the "revelations" concerning the afterlife professed by the New Age movement and the occult? What about spirit guides, séances, and conversations with the dead? Should we seek through these means to explore the hereafter?

God Himself has already given every blood-bought Christian a Guide—the Holy Spirit—but *He* never leads you to contradict the Scriptures. Jesus said, "However, when He, the Spirit of truth, has come, He will guide you into all truth; for He will not speak on His own authority, but whatever He hears He will speak; and He will tell you things to come" (John 16:13). Jesus defined truth when praying to His Father: "Sanctify them by Your truth. *Your word is truth*" (John 17:17, emphasis added).

Listen to Isaiah 8:19–20 (AMPLIFIED) to determine what God thinks about occult activities:

> And when the people [instead of putting their trust in God] shall say to you, Consult for direction mediums and wizards who chirp and mutter, should not a people seek and consult their God? Should they consult the dead on behalf of the living? [Direct such people] to

the teaching and to the testimony [the Scriptures]; if their teachings are not in accord with this word, it is surely because there is no dawn and no morning for them.

The apostle Paul concurred with Isaiah when he wrote these words in Galatians 1:8: "But even if we, or an angel from heaven, preach any other gospel to you than what we have preached to you, let him be accursed."

God wants you to know the truth. He does not want you to fearfully cower in the dark of ignorance, vainly seeking answers in all the wrong places. As John 8:32 indicates, He wants you to know the truth so that the truth can set you free.

God's Word, which is truth, which He honors even above His name, holds the answers to the mysteries of death and the life after. If you are pondering your mortality and are desperate to be immortal, should you not consider its claims?

Embrace it. Let the Word of God become your absolute authority for living as well as for dying. Forsake all other guides and means of exploring the hereafter. To tamper with such will only throw you wide open to the deception and bondage of the devil.

Sally Field, the Academy Award-winning actress, admitted one day on the "Oprah Winfrey Show" her fear of dying. After nearly being killed two years prior in a plane crash, she now lives each day in constant fear of dying, a grim reminder of her own mortality.

Countless multitudes like her are afraid of the dying process and also of death itself because they are unsure of their destination. They ask questions like these: When I die, where will I go? Is the grave my final resting place? Are heaven and hell only old wives' tales or realities? Is there another chance for me in purgatory?

Are there any *real* answers? Yes, in God's Word.

The Grave

A precious elderly friend who was having much trouble reconciling herself to the death of her only daughter finally admitted her turmoil was that she could not help thinking her daughter was still in the grave. The horror of it was almost driving her crazy. When her faithful daughter-in-law discovered the root of the issue, she was able to minister to her the truth of God's Word. As the Scriptures took hold in her heart, the anguish and fear were broken. She knew the truth, and the truth set her free.

When Jesus died upon the cross, we know that His body was buried in a borrowed tomb. But with His last breath He cried, "Father, into Your hands I commit My spirit" (Luke 23:46). We know that according to Scripture, while His body lay in the tomb, His spirit was alive. He went into hell, took the keys to the gates of hell and death from the devil, and fulfilled His promise to the penitent dying thief that He would see him that same day in paradise.

In like manner, Stephen, the first Christian martyr, when being stoned to death cried out, " 'Lord Jesus, receive my spirit.' . . . And when he had said this, he fell asleep" (Acts 7:59–60). Thus, his body died, but his spirit went to be with the Lord.

The death of the believer is described as "falling asleep," but the sleep has reference to the *body* only. Read Ecclesiastes 12:7: "Then the dust [body] will return to the earth as it was, and the spirit will return to God who gave it."

As Clarence Larkin so aptly phrased it, "Death is not a cessation of being. It is simply a cessation of bodily functions that cut off the soul from contact with this present earth. It brings to end this first 'stage' of our existence that we may enter on the second. The cessation of the bodily functions of a man does not include the cessation of his soul functions."

Oh, but, friend, there is coming a time in the future when all the dead in Christ shall rise from their graves. Remember when Jesus arose after being crucified? He arose not just in spirit but also in body—a new resurrection body (see Luke 24:39). A body that would never again experience death; a body that could eat and digest food (see Luke 24:41–43); a body that could walk through walls and appear and disappear at will (see John 20:26).

You, too, who are children of God, will experience this. On that great day when the Lord returns with a shout, the trumpet of the Lord will sound, and the dead in Christ will be resurrected (see 1 Thess. 4:16). Our bodies, whether centuries dead, lost at sea, cremated, or newly buried, will be resurrected from the dust of the earth to join our spirits. Not only are our spirits precious to God, but our bodies are also. They are the tabernacles of the Holy Spirit while we live upon this earth. They are consecrated, holy unto God. They will be resurrected, joined with our spirits, and in a twinkling of an eye changed into resurrection bodies.

Until that day, the shells of our mortal lives will reside in the grave. Our spirits will be alive and active in heaven, waiting. . . .

The Fear of Dying

As a girl, Corrie ten Boom had a fear of dying. She was afraid of what would happen to her if the Nazis discovered that she and her family hid Jews and Christians in the walls of their home to prevent their annihilation by the Third Reich. When she finally admitted this fear to her father, the wise old gentleman asked her this question: "If you were going on a train trip, when would you need the ticket?" "Right before I boarded," Corrie replied. "If I received it any earlier, I might lose it." "Even so," declared her father, "when it comes time to die, at that moment your heavenly Father will give you the ticket, *dying grace.* You'll have it when you need it."

Dear friend, as you have found His grace to be sufficient at the most desperate, devastating times of *life,* even so His grace will be sufficient in *death.* You'll have it when you need it. His grace *is* sufficient.

Purgatory

Purgatory, which means a "place of purification," is never mentioned in the Scriptures. This doctrine was not promulgated until six hundred years after Christ. Believing that few people are fit to go immediately to heaven, churchmen invented an intermediary place where the soul could be purged through physical suffering. The avaricious church of that time, playing upon the fears and sympathies of the bereaved, filled its coffers with revenues from prayers and masses spoken in behalf of the dead. This ungodly doctrine has served to prolong the suffering of the living and is at the same time totally impotent to help the dead. Purgatory is unscriptural.

Heaven or Hell?

The Bible speaks of two places, heaven and hell, where the righteous and the wicked, respectively, are to spend eternity. Larkin says, "The one demands the other. There can be no Heaven without its counterpart Hell. If there is no Hell there is no Heaven, for the same Book speaks of both."

Hell

The Hebrew word *Sheol* is found sixty-five times in the Old Testament. Thirty-one times it is translated "hell"; another thirty-one times, "gravel"; and three times, "the pit." In the Greek New Testament the corresponding word is *hades,* which is translated ten times as "hell." *Sheol* (Old Testament), *hades,* (New Testament), or *hell,* as we now refer to it, is the place to which the soul of the wicked goes after death while the body returns to dust.

In Luke 16, Jesus recounted the insightful narrative of the rich man and Lazarus. The rich man was alive in hell; he was conscious; he could see, hear, speak, and recognize others. He was also tormented in the flames.

Jesus taught that the wicked would be cast into a furnace of fire, where there would be wailing and gnashing of teeth (see Matt. 13:49–50), with their diabolical companions, the devil and his angels (see Matt. 25:41). In Mark 9:42–48, He added more horrifying details—the fire is quenchless, and it contains worms that never die.

Heaven

In marked contrast is heaven, the home and throne of God (see Eccles. 5:2; Isa. 66:1), from which He rules the universe. It is a *place,* not a state or condition, which Jesus has gone to prepare for all those who have loved and obeyed His Father. First Corinthians 2:9 says, "But as it is written, 'Eye has not seen, nor ear heard, nor have entered into the heart of man the things which God has prepared for those who love Him.'" The book of Revelation gives us a sneak preview: fruit trees beside the river of life, streets of gold, unsurpassed music, no night, no tears, and no separation from the presence of God, for He will live among us.

"Some people live in fear of death (Hebrews 2:15)," says Larkin, "and cannot bear to think of it, but those of us who know that Heaven is to be our Eternal Home ought not to fear 'Death,' for it is 'Death' that opens the door for our 'Exodus' from earth to glory."

Pilgrims

According to Hebrews 11:10–13, the Old Testament patriarch Abraham was looking for a city whose builder and maker was God, knowing that he was a stranger and pilgrim on this earth. That is, as the old gospel song says,

> This world is not my home,
> I'm just a'passin' through.

39

My treasures are laid up
Somewhere beyond the blue.
The angels beckon me
From heaven's open door,
And I can't feel at home
In this world anymore!

In November 1989, Lynn Hilinski's daughter, Jill, was struck with an aneurysm to the brain and died. She was two weeks away from her eighteenth birthday. Lynn later testified, "How we act or react to situations is up to us. But God is a good God, and He gave us a good and perfect gift in Jill for the years that we enjoyed her. Now, I can hardly wait for the day when I am going to be with her. . . . This world is not my home."

Jill was just "a pilgrim here below." Now her family more clearly understands about "treasure laid up in heaven."

My mother has suffered the loss of her entire family to death: a brother and a sister who died as small children while she was only a girl, two adult brothers, a very dear sister, and her mother and father. In her eighty years, she has lost many close friends to death as well. But each death served to deepen the reality of heaven to her. Throughout my life, she has often talked of heaven not as some mystical, ethereal *un*reality but as an actual city where a multitude of her loved ones now live and where she will be moving to join them someday.

The Valley of the Shadow

One of the most comforting verses in all the Bible is Psalm 23:4:

Yea, though I walk through the valley of the shadow of death,
I will fear no evil;
For You are with me.

The patriarch Job, King David, the prophets Jeremiah and Amos, and Dr. Luke all referred to death as "the valley of the shadow." Let me ask you, can a shadow hurt you? When an airplane flies overhead and the shadow falls across the ground, can that shadow injure you? When you are sitting at a railroad crossing and the shadow of the passing train touches your car, do you feel any impact? No, of course not. It is only a shadow, a shadow of a real thing. Likewise, death for the child of God is only a shadow of the real thing. Those who experience the "real thing" are those who depart this life without a personal faith in the person and blood of Jesus Christ as their only means of salvation. Physical death is the door that ushers them into the reality of *eternal* death.

But for the believing child of God, the journey through the valley of the shadow can be glorious, not fearful. I like the term *pass* used more frequently in years gone by. Hebrews 4:14 notes that Jesus Himself has "passed through the heavens." Instead of thinking that when you come to the end of your earthly life, you are going to die—which sounds so *final* and invokes fear—think that you are going to "pass." Although this sounds simplistic, it was the very word that freed me from the fear of dying. One day I realized that I was never going to die. The eternal life of God was breathed into my spirit when I repented of my sins and received Jesus as my Lord and Savior, and I would never die. I would only pass—pass out of this imperfect, limited, feeble clay tabernacle of a body into the presence of God.

I want to share with you a passage from Clarence Larkin's little book *The Spirit World* about our first experiences after death:

> Did you ever stop to think of what happens to the Righteous Soul during the first five minutes after death? Before the funeral has been held, and the body laid away in the cemetery, nay, before the undertaker has been sent for, or the neighbors and relatives notified, or the shades drawn, or the silent watchers at the bedside have realized that you are dead you have been FIVE MINUTES out of the body and reached Paradise and know where you are to spend eternity. Now what will be our experiences in those first five minutes? (1) Our first experience will be that death was so easy. That it was like falling asleep and awakening in a beautiful world. That there were no hobgoblins, satyrs, and demons to traverse, no "dark river" to cross, but that "Ministering Angels" were waiting to convey us to Paradise as they carried Lazarus. Luke 16:22. . . . (2) Our second experience will be the consciousness that we have left behind our earthly body with all its weaknesses, sufferings, and limitations, and have a body that is absolutely well and fitted in every way for the spiritual realm in which it is to dwell. (3) Our third experience will be that we are being transported swiftly upward through the ethereal space toward a beautiful country whose radiance is brighter than the sun. . . . (4) Our fourth experience will be that we are in a new environment whose atmosphere is LOVE. That there is no discord, or lack of harmony in our new home, and that its chief characteristic is HOLINESS.

(5) Our fifth experience will be the feeling that we are near Jesus. If we do not actually see Him, we shall have the consciousness of His nearness. (6) Our sixth experience will be that of meeting our loved ones. . . . (7) Our seventh experience will be the meeting with the saints who have preceded us to glory, such as the patriarchs, prophets, apostles and Christian leaders of our own day. The experiences named may not all happen in the first five minutes after death, but they doubtless will happen before our funeral service is over and our body laid to rest in the tomb.

Surely, as the psalmist wrote, "Precious in the sight of the LORD is the death of His saints" (Ps. 116:15).

My mother's father was an invalid for thirty-three years with rheumatoid arthritis. Every other Saturday, my mother, daddy, and I would make the hour-long drive to see him and Gran. Even though many years have passed, I distinctly remember the last Saturday we spent with him because of the unusual circumstances surrounding it. All day long I remember Papa saying to my grandmother, "Cora, turn up the radio. There's such beautiful music playing today!" Gran, in perplexity, replied, "Andy, the radio's not on!" "But it is!" he would almost shout. "I can hear it, and oh, it is the most beautiful music I've ever heard. Turn it up!"

This scene was repeated several times during the day, and each time Papa became increasingly frustrated with everyone because no one would do as he said and turn up the music! The next morning when Gran awakened and went to check on him, she discovered that Papa was no longer there. He had "passed" during the night. Ministering angels (see Heb. 1:14) had come to welcome and convey him safely into his Father's house.

When Lottie Moon, the faithful Southern Baptist missionary to China, lay dying, her last hours were spent more in the other world than this one. Propped up on pillows, with her hands pressed together in the customary Chinese greeting, she bowed to one friend after another who came to meet her as she entered her new home. Each friend she called by name. Each friend was a Chinese believer who had preceded her in death.

The great Chicago preacher of last century, Dwight L. Moody, wanted to be remembered in this fashion:

Some day you will read in the papers that D. L. Moody, of East Northfield, is dead. Don't you believe a word of it! At that moment

I shall be more alive than I am now. I shall have gone up higher, that is all; gone out of this old clay tenement into a house that is immortal, a body that death cannot touch, that sin cannot taint, a body like unto His own glorious body. I was born of the flesh in 1837. I was born of the Spirit in 1855. That which is born of the flesh may die. That which is born of the Spirit will live forever.

As A. P. Fitt, his son-in-law and biographer, wrote, "He firmly believed to the last that the opening portals of Heaven would only admit him to larger and truer service for his God and Saviour in unseen worlds."

In his last remaining hours in this life, Moody, too, experienced the beginnings of eternity, which were witnessed by his family and chronicled by Fitt:

"Earth recedes; Heaven opens before me," he cried. "No, this is no dream. . . . It is beautiful! It is like a trance! If this is death, it is sweet! There is no valley here! God is calling me, and I must go!"

Then it seemed as though he saw beyond the veil, for he exclaimed: "This is my triumph; this is my coronation day! I have been looking forward to it for years."

Then his face lit up, and he said, in a voice of joyful rapture, "Dwight! Irene! I see the children's faces!" referring to his two little grandchildren, whom God had taken home within the past year.

Later, he feebly uttered these words: "No pain! No valley! . . . If this is death, it's not bad at all! It's *sweet!*"

When it comes time for you to walk through the shadow we call Death, if you are a child of God, you will not have to fear any evil. The promise of God is, "I will never leave you nor forsake you," particularly at such an important time of transition. In heaven your angels always behold the face of the Father (see Matt. 18:10), and He has given them charge over you to keep you in all of your ways (see Ps. 91:11). As you go through the valley of the shadow, your guardian angels will be your guiding companions through the celestial realms and into the home of your Father.

Desperate to Be Immortal

Whether you are a child of God or not, there is an everlasting existence of the soul. You will shed your body at some point in the future, much like a butterfly sheds its cocoon. If you have given your life unreservedly to God, trusting only in the blood and righteousness of Jesus for your salvation, you'll pass into everlasting life. If this has not been your choice in life, you'll pass into everlasting damnation. Do you know for certain which your future holds?

Second Peter 3:9 teaches that it is not God's will for anyone to perish but for all to come to repentance. Jesus left the comfort of heaven for you. He gave His life willingly for you. He defeated Satan and broke the power of death for you. He arose victorious over death, hell, and the grave for you. He is now seated at the right hand of God the Father interceding for you. He loves you.

He wants you to know for certain whether or not you belong to Him. He does not want you to wonder or linger in doubt over the most crucial issues of life.

The apostle John wrote in his first epistle, "He who has the Son has life; he who does not have the Son of God does not have life. These things I have written to you . . . *that you may know* that you have eternal life, and that you may . . . believe in the name of the Son of God" (5:12–13, emphasis added).

Have you exchanged your life for His; your sin and shame for His forgiveness and integrity; your guilt for His confident love; your confusion for His peace? The exchange is a wonderful one. In it Jesus takes all your wretchedness and gives you all His wholeness, your death for His life.

Jesus said, "I am the way, the truth, and the life. No one comes to the Father except through Me" (John 14:6). Apart from Jesus, you have no way of entering into eternal life with God: "But as many as received Him, to them He gave the right to become children of God, to those who believe on His name" (John 1:12).

"But," you may say, "what will my friends and family say?" Dear one, when you stand before the God of the whole earth and give an account of the decisions you have made while below, excuses such as, "I couldn't give my life to Jesus because of what my friends would have said," will be pretty lame. Your friends won't be able to come to your defense at that moment. They will need one of their own. In that instant, it will just be you and Him. It will be too late to wish that you had dealt with the doubts concerning your eternal destiny while you still had time. Time will be no more.

Many years ago I went through a terrible period of doubt over whether or not I really was a child of God. I had been reared in a wonderful Christian home and had had spiritual experiences at different times in my life. Later, I married Larry, and we were serving in a pastoral position on a church staff. But through some bad teaching, a spirit of fear and condemnation gripped my soul. I lost the joy of the Lord; I doubted my salvation; I feared the future. Finally, at my most intense time of desperation after months of despondency, I shut myself away from everyone, determined to find out from God if, indeed, I belonged to Him. I humbled myself. It did not matter that I knew reams of Bible minutiae, that everyone thought I was a wonderful example of a Christian wife and mother. I needed to know *from God* where I stood with Him. I needed to know the truth so that it could set me free. I was even willing for the truth to be awful. I had decided that if the Lord told me that I had never really been born again, I would simply humble myself and ask Him to save me instead of debating my righteousness. I had nothing to lose in facing the truth but everything to gain.

As I brokenly poured out my heart to God, the comfort of the Holy Spirit came upon me as physically as a warm blanket about my shoulders. He bore witness in my heart that I was indeed a child of God; that my sins were forgiven; that I was on my way to heaven.

My point in telling this personal incident is to say to you, ask God what is the truth of your spiritual condition. If you don't know the truth, it can't set you free. If you are not a child of God, repent of your sins and receive Jesus. If you are unsure, humble yourself and ask God if you belong to Him. Don't be afraid; *be sure*. Take courage. Get it settled once and for all.

Today, right now, won't you lay all your fears and doubts and unbelief at the feet of Jesus? Won't you turn your whole life unreservedly over to the One who loves you and gave Himself for you?

"Whosoever will may come" is the call issued by God. His promise is, "The one who comes to Me I will by no means cast out" (John 6:37).

If you are desperate to be immortal, you can find it only in Jesus Christ.

Dr. L. Nelson Bell said, "Only those who are prepared to die are really prepared to live."

What about you?

7 Desperate to Have an Identity

". . . Hallowed be Your name."

Only as we know who God is and who we are in Him can we really know who we are and what we're good for.

—Melva Lea

You are complete in Him.

—Colossians 2:10

Rockwall, Texas, is a suburban community twenty miles east of Dallas on the shores of Lake Ray Hubbard. We are joined to Dallas by two mile-long bridges that span the lake. One bright sunny morning in 1980 as I started across the first bridge, life was wonderful. I was Melva Lea, college graduate, pastor's wife, chief chauffeur for John, Jo Anna, and Joy, primary food distributor for Tuffy (the dog) and Puddy Tat (our half-blind, epileptic cat), avid gardener of trees, bushes, and shrubs Texas-style (dry, withered, sunburned brown, or dead altogether from the yearly three-day, near-zero winter freeze). I mean, come on now, I knew who I was.

But by the time I reached the other end of the first bridge I was in tears. "Who *am* I? What am I good for?" I blubbered to God. "*Apart* from Larry, *apart* from the kids, *apart* from all my *doing*. Who am *I?*"

Have you ever acted so strangely?

My excuse was that I was in a season of transition. One week I was twenty-nine years old, the wife of a past-youth-minister-now-evangelist. The next week I was thirty, the wife of the senior pastor of a fledgling church with women coming to me saying, "When are we going to start a ladies' ministry?"

A ladies' ministry? (Silent scream!) Are you kidding? How can I help *you*? Today, I don't even know who *I* am. I just discovered *yesterday* that I wasn't a teenager anymore and wonder what I've been doing for the last ten years. Now, suddenly, I'm supposed to have answers for your life's questions? HELP!!

As I've said before, TRANSITION IS THE PITS! It is a time of change, a time of shaking, a time when everything that was once familiar is replaced with the unknown brand-new. A time when what you thought you *knew* is not applicable anymore. A time when you question everything. A time when you awaken one day and with panic in your voice say, "I'm having an identity crisis."

The world will tell you that you can be self-assured and confident if you'll only wear the right fragrance; have matching eyeshadow, blush, lipstick, and nail polish; look like the seventeen-year-old model in the magazine (who has never had three babies!); use mouthwash and deodorant; and chew the right gum.

Oh, come on! We women need something that's going to last longer than denture cement and be more substantial than the last pay raise. We want something more dependable than antilock brakes and more reliable than waterproof mascara.

We are not complete in Calvin Klein, Ralph Lauren, or even a dozen other men. We are complete only in *Him*—Jesus (see Col. 2:10)!

Only as we know who God is and who we are in Him can we really know who we are and what we're good for.

But a twofold problem exists: very few people really *know* God, and only after many years of disappointing attempts at relationships, careers, and TV offers do most women of the last few generations "find themselves."

During World War II the men went to war, and the women went to work. Up until that time, woman's primary place had been in the home. But after the war, many women found that they liked their independence, an additional income, and the sense of self-worth they obtained from a career, and so they continued in the work force. Then began a gradual, steady increase in divorces nationwide until by the end of the eighties, one out of every two marriages ended in divorce. Multitudes of others chose not to tie the ceremonial knot, preferring not to make promises that obviously only a few were willing to keep.

Men and women were victims of the times, but so were several generations of children, children who grew up in multiple families, who seldom lived to adulthood with their original set of parents. In the "olden days" children were nurtured by their immediate family and usually were surrounded by grandmothers, aunts, and cousins of their extended family; today it's a different story. We are no longer a "Leave It to Beaver" society with Mom, Dad, Wally, and Beaver. The American family of the nineties is usually fragmented. A mind-boggling number of children are latchkey kids. This may be reminiscent of your upbringing or the way in which your own children are growing up. No condemnation here. Just the observation that for the most part we are a society without emotional roots. We don't know who we are, what we're good for, or where we're going. It takes our older children five to seven years longer now to leave home because they lack these answers.

Matthew 13:3–6 illustrates where many of us are today:

> [Jesus] spoke many things to them in parables, saying: "Behold, a sower went out to sow. And as he sowed, some seed . . . fell on stony places, where they did not have much earth; and they immediately sprang up because they had no depth of earth. But when the sun was up they were scorched, and *because they had no root* they withered away" (emphasis added).

Verses 20–21 further explain: "But he who received the seed on stony places, this is he who hears the word and immediately receives it with joy; yet he has *no root in himself,* but endures only for a while. For when tribulation or persecution arises because of the word, immediately he stumbles" (emphasis added).

Instead of being like a well-tended garden, you may have grown up like a field full of weeds, making it the best way you could. Often the "nurturing" some of you received was worse than none at all. "You'll never amount to anything"; "Why can't you be more like your sister?"; "I wish you'd never been born"; "Why don't you just quit?"—these and a multitude of other negative comments only stifled and rendered ineffective healthy growth.

But even if your upbringing was positive, and you are generally secure in yourself, the winds of change blow across you every day. With negative words and actions constantly bombarding you from the devil and other people, unless your security comes from the Lord, it, too, will fail you. Without God-given root in yourself, you'll be sunburned and withered by the heat of life, unfruitful and spiritually barren, easily offended when your expectations of God don't measure up to your present reality. Without root in yourself, you will not have had a lifetime of victorious experiences learning to overcome impossibilities and endure to the finish line. Without root in yourself, when the devil attacks you as you're trying to stand in faith on the Word of God, you will not have enough spiritual character developed to discern his wiles but will instead become offended, blaming God.

We all know people who received the good news with joy, but then, one day, we looked up, and they were nowhere to be found. Later we learned how they had become offended over some spiritual issue, dropped out of sight, and are yet to resurface.

Maybe this is not someone else's story; perhaps this is what has happened to you. Ecclesiastes 9:4 says where there is life, there is hope. If you are still breathing as you read these words, there is still time to develop root in yourself that will forever change the way you perceive yourself and your relationship with God.

But this work does not occur through futile "striving in the flesh." *You cannot develop root in yourself by looking at yourself. You develop root in yourself only by looking at God.*

Paul wrote, "Not that we are sufficient of ourselves to think of anything as being from ourselves, but our sufficiency is from God. . . . But we all, with unveiled face, beholding as in a mirror the glory of the Lord, are being transformed into the same image from glory to glory, just as by the Spirit of the Lord" (2 Cor. 3:5, 18).

Your job is to "behold" Him, worshiping Him for who He is. His job is to change you from glory to glory, conforming you into the image of Jesus. Consequently, when you pray daily according to the pattern given by Jesus, you do not hallow your name, you *hallow the name of God.* He is everything you are not; He is everything you have need of. He alone is complete within Himself, and you are in desperate need of His identity, His completeness to be manifest in your incompleteness.

Jehovah, the familiar name of God used by the Israelites, is translated, "I AM WHO I AM" (Ex. 3:14). God has no difficulty with His identity. He knows who He was, who He is, and who He will be. He *AM*—personal, continuous, absolute. He has given you hope of stability and security with His words, "I am Jehovah; I change not." He is your rock that never rolls, your fortress that never falls. He is permanent. As Nathan Stone has written in his book *Names of God,*

> To Israel of old righteousness and holiness were the two great attributes associated with the name Jehovah. . . . It is this righteousness of Jehovah against which man sins. And a righteous Jehovah whose holiness is thus violated and outraged must condemn unrighteousness and punish it. So it is Jehovah who pronounces judgment and metes out punishment. . . . But as Jehovah He is also Love. His love makes Him grieve and suffer for the sins and sorrows of His creatures. . . . But while, as Jehovah, His holiness must condemn, He is also Love, and His love redeems; and He seeks to bring man back into fellowship with Himself. So as one writer says: "Wherever the name 'Jehovah' appears, after man has fallen from original righteousness, what see we—but that God is ever seeking the restoration of man."

Even so, God is seeking your restoration, your completeness in Him. That as you look unto Him, you'll be filled with His righteousness, not your own; that your sin will be rooted out and your way made straight so that you might enjoy His fellowship and have confidence in His presence; that you'll daily experience the redeeming power of His unfathomable love, the deep serenity that comes from knowing experientially that you are the delight of His heart.

He is absolute, unshakable, immovable. Do you realize what this means to you? Nothing that happens in your life will ever catch Him off guard or unprepared. He'll still be right in the same place waiting for you to come talk it over with Him, wanting to help you.

He is righteous. As you behold Him, worshiping Him for who He is, you will be changed. He will impute righteousness to you through the blood of Jesus. *He is just* and judges sin. As you behold Him, He, in mercy, will reveal to you the sin of your heart so that you can receive forgiveness. Then He will draw you to Himself, free from condemnation, to enter into the love and joy of the Lord.

And thus, you are changed from glory to glory, from faith to faith. Looking to Him, confronting what He shows you and allowing Him to deal with it, changing you into the image of Christ—therein, you will find your true identity.

Throughout the centuries of the Bible, God progressively revealed Himself to His people so that they might more fully understand Him and become more like Him. In like manner, as you behold Him through His names, you will understand Him more fully and be changed. You will know Him in a dimension you've never before experienced, and day by day, you will develop root in yourself.

Who Is God?

Jehovah-Jireh (je-ho'-vah yeer'-eh)—
The Lord Our Provider

The name *Jehovah-Jireh* comes from one of the most exciting stories in the Old Testament. In Genesis 22 it is recorded that Abraham was commanded by God to offer his son Isaac as a burnt sacrifice on Mount Moriah. Abraham—knowing that it was not God's nature to require human sacrifice as did the other heathen nations round about him but also believing that God had the power to raise Isaac from the dead—proceeded to obey the Lord. Just as the knife was being raised to kill Isaac, the Lord commanded Abraham to stop. The Lord provided a ram, caught by its horns in the bushes, as the sacrifice instead of Isaac. Through this incident we see Abraham's obedience and faith, Isaac's willing submission, and Jehovah's gracious provision of a substitute in his place. Genesis 22:14 states, "And Abraham called the name of the place, The-LORD-Will-Provide [Jehovah-Jireh]." *Jireh* comes from the verb "to see," so Jehovah-Jireh is the One who sees what you have need of and provides the answer to that need. Jesus said in Matthew 6:8, "Your Father knows the things you have need of before you ask Him."

While Abraham and Isaac were climbing up one side of the mountain going to the place of sacrifice, God was sending a ram up the other! God knew the need even before Abraham and Isaac did and had already provided the answer.

Isaac represented all mankind needing a substitute to die in its place. Jesus is the picture of the ram, the substitute sacrifice provided by God—the only One whose blood can take away your sin. The same Lord, who has provided for your salvation, will also take care of your other needs.

What is your need today? Do you lack finances? Look to the Lord, Jehovah-Jireh. He gives you the ability to make wealth (see Deut. 8:18). Do you need food, clothes, the basic necessities of life? His promise in Matthew 6:25-33 is summed up with, "But seek first the kingdom of God and His righteousness, and all these things shall be added to you." Do you need friends? Listen to this encouragement: "Every good gift and every perfect gift is from above, and comes down from the Father" (James 1:17).

Do you need family? His promise to you is Psalm 68:5-6:

A father of the fatherless, a defender of widows,
Is God in His holy habitation.
God sets the solitary in families.

And so on. Whatever your need, God is your Provider. Worship Him for who He is, your faithful Provider. You are complete in Him.

Jehovah-Rophe (je-ho'-vah ro'-phay)— The Lord Our Healer

Exodus 15:22–26 provides the backdrop for the name *Jehovah-Rophe*. The children of Israel had just passed through the Red Sea after a miraculous deliverance from Egypt. They had seen God do great signs and wonders to bring about their deliverance from the hand of Pharaoh. Now they were three days' journey past the Red Sea, into the Wilderness, and no water was to be found. Finally, they came to Marah and discovered water, but "they could not drink the waters of Marah, for they were bitter. Therefore the name of it was called Marah [which means bitter]" (v. 23).

You can imagine how relieved the Israelites were to find water, and then how disappointed and angry they became when they discovered it could not be consumed. When the children of Israel began to criticize Moses, he cried out to God, and the Lord showed him a tree that when cut down and put into the waters made them sweet! Then God spoke, "If you diligently heed the voice of the LORD your God and do what is right in His sight, give ear to His commandments and keep all His statutes, I will put none of the diseases on you which I have brought on the Egyptians. For I am the LORD who heals you [Jehovah-Rophe]."

Out of this terrible experience in the Wilderness, Israel learned another new and comforting name of God. During your times of wilderness and desperation, you, too, can experience in greater measure than ever before the healing hand of God. The tree that Moses cut down and cast into the waters represents the Lord Jesus. Your soul is made foul and bitter by sin, even as the waters of Marah. Your body may suffer from sickness and disease. But when God puts His Son, Jesus (the tree), into the bitter waters of your life, everything is changed, and life becomes sweet. Healing is possible.

God's desire for you is that you be well in body, soul, and spirit. The blood of Jesus was shed that spiritually you could be healed by being forgiven of your sins. His blood was also spilled that healing could be provided for your body and soul (mind, will, and emotions). The translation of Isaiah 53:4–5 says,

> Surely He has borne our griefs
> And carried our sorrows. . . .
> But He was wounded for our transgressions,
> He was bruised for our iniquities;
> The chastisement of our peace was upon Him,
> And by His stripes we are healed.

As the old gospel hymn says, "Jesus paid it *all*."

Matthew recorded, "When the evening had come, they brought to Him many who were demon-possessed. And He cast out the spirits with a word, and healed all who were sick, that it might be fulfilled which was spoken by Isaiah the prophet, saying: 'He Himself took our infirmities and bore our sicknesses'" (8:16–17).

The apostle Peter also confirmed this when he wrote, "Who Himself bore our sins in His own body on the tree, that we, having died to sins, might live for righteousness—by whose stripes you were healed" (1 Peter 2:24).

Jesus has already suffered to pay for your healing. It is your Father's will that you be whole. But is your body plagued with discomfort and disease? Are you tormented in your mind? Is your identity locked up in infirmity? Remember Jehovah-Rophe. He is the Lord who heals you. He forgives all your iniquities and heals all your diseases. He redeems your life from destruction and crowns you with lovingkindness and tender mercies. He satisfies your mouth with good things so that your youth is renewed like the eagle's. He is the very strength of your life and soundness to all your flesh.

Worship Him for who He is, your Healer. You are complete in Him.

Jehovah-Nissi (je-ho'-vah nis'-see)— The Lord, My Banner

Only a few weeks had passed since Israel had left Marah, the place of bitter waters. Next they journeyed to Rephidim, the place where Jehovah would reveal Himself as Jehovah-Nissi, their banner of protection. Israel came into confrontation with the Amalekites, distant relatives who, instead of being friendly, were a constant menace and enemy.

Moses gave this command to Joshua: "Choose us some men and go out, fight with Amalek. Tomorrow I will stand on the top of the hill with the rod of God in my hand" (Ex. 17:9).

So Joshua and his men fought with the Amalekites; Moses, Aaron, and Hur went up on the mountain. When Moses held up his hand with the rod of God in it (the same one he used to open the Red Sea), the Israelites won over their enemies. But when his arms grew weary and he lowered them, the Amalekites prevailed. So Aaron and Hur stood on each side of Moses and held up his arms until the sun set. Thus, Joshua and Israel defeated their enemy.

Then Moses built an altar and called its name "The Lord-Is-My-Banner" (Jehovah-Nissi).

A banner in ancient times was not necessarily a flag such as we use nowadays. Often it was a pole. In this particular incident, the banner was the rod of God. As Israel's warriors looked to it, they were reminded that *victory would come through God and God alone,* even as at the Red Sea. They realized that as long as His banner was raised, victory was assured. They knew Jehovah as provider and healer and also as protector.

Jesus is the rod prophesied by Isaiah who would grow out of the stem of Jesse. His death on the cross revealed God's mighty power to redeem your soul. Through God the Father's covering banner of love over your life, He commissioned Jesus to conquer the enemy of your soul, the devil. Daily you can experience victory as you put your trust in Him. Ephesians 1:19–22 tells you that Jesus has been placed far above all principalities and power and might and dominion and every name that is named. Jesus is Lord over all!

Whatever threatens to destroy you, whatever fears torment you, God has lifted up His banner, Jesus, in your behalf. He is your covering of love and protection, your mighty warrior fighting the enemy on your behalf. He promised, "I will contend with him who contends with you" (Isa. 49:25). Put your faith in Him. Call upon His name. Believe that, as Martin Luther wrote in "A Mighty Fortress Is Our God," "the right man" is on your side:

> The Man of God's own choosing:
> Dost ask who that may be?
> Christ Jesus it is He;
> Lord Sabaoth His Name,
> From age to age the same,
> And He must win the battle.

If God be for you, who can be against you? For "we are more than conquerors through Him who loved us" (Rom. 8:31, 37). And you should join in proclaiming, "Thanks be to God, who gives us the victory through our Lord Jesus Christ" (1 Cor. 15:57).

Worship Him for who He is, your Banner. You are complete in Him.

Jehovah-M'Kaddesh (je-ho'-vah m'kad'-desh)— The Lord Who Sanctifies

Abraham had to come to know the Lord as Jehovah-Jireh, his Provider; Israel, too, came to understand this in the Passover lamb, their substitute for sin that God had provided. They grew to know Him at the waters of Marah as Jehovah-Rophe, the One who heals the bitter times in life and is also the Great Physician. Then Israel came to know Him at Rephidim as Jehovah-Nissi, the Lord their Banner, their Protector during times of battle.

Now the Israelites were coming to a new land—the land promised them by God. But it was full of many nations of people, people with wicked and cruel customs who worshiped other gods. Knowing that people become like the gods they serve, God said to Moses, "Speak to all the congregation of the children of Israel, and say to them, 'You shall be holy, for I the LORD your God am holy'" (Lev. 19:2). Then He revealed a new name to them: "I am Jehovah-M'Kaddesh, the LORD who sanctifies you" (Lev. 20:8).

God wanted His people to show forth His glory and not learn the ways of neighboring nations that sacrificed their children in fire to false gods and committed other heinous sins.

God wanted His people to be holy, set apart unto Him and His purposes. God who cannot look upon sin or have any fellowship with it knew that if His people did not choose to live holy, they would be cut off, separated from His presence and His protection. He wanted the very best for them: He wanted them to be blessed, but they had to choose to be separated unto Him, sanctified, holy.

It is the same with you and me today. Sin breaks our fellowship with God. It grieves His heart; it separates us from His presence.

You have been chosen by God to be His; Jesus has already paid for your salvation and sanctification. Now you must daily choose to live holy. Jesus Himself had to choose. It is recorded of Jesus: "Behold, I have come to do *Your* will, O God" (Heb. 10:9, emphasis added). You must remember that you are not your own. You are bought with a price. Therefore glorify God in your body, which is His temple. Romans 12:1-2 says, "I beseech you therefore, [sisters], by the mercies of God, that you present your bodies a living sacrifice, holy, acceptable to God, which is your reasonable service. And do not be conformed to this world, but be transformed by the renewing of your mind, that you may prove what is that good and acceptable and perfect will of God." First Corinthians 3:16-17 continues the image: "Do you not know that you are the temple of God and that the Spirit of God dwells in you? If anyone defiles the temple of God, God will destroy him. For the temple of God is holy, which temple you are."

When you receive Jesus as Lord, the Spirit of God comes and indwells you. Your body is no longer your own—it is His house. What is going on at your address in *His* house? Are you treating His dwelling place with honor and respect? Are you taking care of it in such a manner that it will bring Him glory for a long time?

To live holy is to live happy. Holiness has usually been associated with a bunch of do's and don'ts. But the Holy Spirit does not hold a stick over your head like some people you've known or perhaps a religious organization in which you've had membership. He frees you from the sins and weights that weigh you down and take the joy out of your life. He brings you into a living relationship with God your Father, which brings a wholeness to your identity.

Often other people attempt to help the Holy Spirit. They think He's some nonentity who's just mentioned in the Bible. They don't really believe that He is a real person who has come to convict of sin, righteousness, and judgment and also to comfort and guide into all truth. So they presume to become your "Holy Spirit" and tell you what you can and cannot do, what's "holy" and what's not. Usually they cause you to think that anything associated with holiness is unattractive, unexciting, and impossible for a human being to live.

Holiness does not begin with an outward show—holiness begins with the heart. As you grow in your love of God, as you more fully understand and obey His Word and His ways, the Holy Spirit will gently guide you to be and live pleasing unto the Lord. On occasion He will whisper to you, "This is the way. Walk in it." Another time He may say, "This particular thought (or activity) is a weight to you. Lay it down." And yet another time He may be very straightforward with you: "What you're doing is working death in you! Stop it!" But He always works with redemption in mind: redeeming your life from destruction; bringing you out of darkness into light; filling your heart with righteousness, peace, joy, and abundance of *life*—for *real!* After all, His thoughts and ways are higher than yours. And only He knows what will give you true fulfillment and abundance of life.

One of my favorite scriptural promises is Philippians 2:13: "For it is God who works in you both to will and to do for His good pleasure." It comforts me to know that the Holy Spirit will begin to work in my will so that I will *want* to do HIS will. Then when my "want to" gets right, He works in my "doer" the ability to actually accomplish His will.

He is working in you both to *will* and to *do* that you might daily grow in holiness and be well pleasing to Him; that you might experience the heights of joy in unbroken, untainted friendship with Him.

Worship Him for who He is, your Sanctifier. You are complete in Him.

Jehovah-Shalom (je-ho'-vah shal-lom')—
The Lord Our Peace

The name of *Jehovah-Shalom* appears in Judges 6:24. It had been two hundred years since God had revealed Himself to Israel as Jehovah-M'Kaddesh, the Lord their Sanctifier. After the death of Joshua, the nation turned from God. Every person lived by what was right in his own eyes, not according to the commandments of God. They began to adopt the heathen practices of nations round about them and worship their gods. Consequently, the blessing of the Lord departed from them, and Israel became a constant victim of the plunder and destruction of invading hordes. At that particular time, Israel was enslaved to the Midianites.

A young man named Gideon was hiding in a winepress, threshing wheat salvaged from the last attack of the enemy. Suddenly the Angel of the Lord appeared to him, saying, "The LORD is with you, you mighty man of valor!" (Judg. 6:12). He commanded Gideon, "Go in this might of yours, and you shall save Israel from the hand of the Midianites. Have I not sent you?" (Judg. 6:14).

Talk about an identity crisis! This pronouncement caused Gideon great consternation of soul. He saw himself differently from what the Lord did. In his own eyes he was a nobody. His clan was the smallest in his tribe, and he was the youngest in his father's house. Who was he to deliver the children of Israel from the domination of Midian?

But the Lord saw a man who had a heart to obey His commands.

57

The Lord said to him, "Surely I will be with you, and you shall defeat the Midianites as one man" (Judg. 6:16).

All at once Gideon perceived that he was talking with Jehovah. He feared because he knew Jehovah was holy, while Gideon and all Israel were unrighteous. Then Gideon said, "If it is really *You*, I must prepare a sacrifice."

As Gideon prepared his offering, the Lord touched it with the staff in His hand and fire rose up out of the rock altar, consuming the sacrifice. Then the Lord said to him, "Peace be with you: do not fear, you shall not die" (Judg. 6:23).

Judges 6:24 records that Gideon built an altar there to the Lord and called it The-Lord-Shalom, confident that God would give Israel victory over the Midianites and peace to their land.

Peace comes through obedience. When the people of Israel had sanctified themselves, obeying the commandments of the Lord, they had experienced God's provision, health, and protection. But when they left Him, they left the source of their peace. Gideon realized that because he had received the command from the Lord and was determined to obey it, peace would be his, and all Israel's, too.

Jesus is your peace; He has broken down all the walls separating you from God (see Eph. 2:14). Believe it! He broke down those walls with the breaking of His own body and shedding of His own blood on your behalf. As you daily receive forgiveness of your sins through the blood already appropriated, you can experience daily peace. Jesus is the Prince of Peace, and through Him, the peace of God, which passes all understanding, shall keep your heart and mind (see Phil. 4:7).

When you're tempted to worry or become anxious or berate yourself about how worthless you are, obey instead Colossians 3:15: "Let the peace of God rule in your [heart]."

Worship Jehovah-Shalom for who He is, and *let* His peace rule you today. Remember, you are complete in Him.

Jehovah-Tsidkenu (je-ho'-vah tsid-kay'-noo)— The Lord Our Righteousness

Hundreds of years had passed since Gideon had come to know God as Jehovah-Shalom, but the spiritual condition of the nation of Israel was even worse than it had been in his time. Ten of the twelve tribes of Israel had finally been carried off into slavery, never to be heard of again. Conditions for the remaining tribe of Judah went from bad to worse. Kings, priests, and people alike worshiped other gods and practiced abominations.

During this period of gross national sin, God called a young prophet, Jeremiah, to proclaim His word once again to the backslidden nation. The Lord said to Jeremiah,

> "Before I formed you in the womb I knew you;
> Before you were born I sanctified you;
> I ordained you a prophet to the nations."

Then said I:

> "Ah, Lord GOD!
> Behold, I cannot speak, for I am a youth."

But the LORD said to me:

> "Do not say, 'I am a youth,'
> For you shall go to all to whom I send you,
> And whatever I command you, you shall speak.
> Do not be afraid of their faces,
> For I am with you to deliver you" (Jer. 1:5–8).

Jeremiah spent his whole life speaking the word of the Lord to the people of Judah, urging them to repent, but they would not. Jeremiah prophesied another King who was of the same heart toward God as David and who would inherit his throne:

> "Behold, the days are coming," says the LORD,
> "That I will raise to David a Branch of righteousness;
> A King shall reign and prosper,
> And execute judgment and righteousness in the earth.
> In His days Judah will be saved,
> And Israel will dwell safely;
> Now this is His name by which He will be called:
> THE LORD OUR RIGHTEOUSNESS [Jehovah-Tsidkenu]"
>
> (Jer. 23:5–6).

Jeremiah did not know that his prophecy would not be fulfilled until several hundred years later when a baby, born in a manger in Bethlehem, would become that righteous King and lead His people once again in holiness. That holiness was possible only after a "divine exchange." Jesus, Jehovah-Tsidkenu, paid your penalty for sin with His death on the cross. Jesus, who had no sin in Him, became sin for you so that you could become righteous by Him (see 2 Cor. 5:21). *He took your sin and gave you His righteousness* so that you could be right with God.

If you derive your identity from how hard you work for God to be accepted by Him, you are wasting your energy. God is not impressed with your "righteousness." Remember what Isaiah called it? "Filthy rags." God is impressed only with the blood of Jesus. It alone, applied daily to your sins, gives you entrance into His presence. It alone is your righteousness. As the old hymn says,

> This is all my hope and peace,
> Nothing but the blood of Jesus;
> This is all my righteousness,
> Nothing but the blood of Jesus.
>
> Oh! precious is the flow
> That makes me white as snow;
> No other fount I know,
> Nothing but the blood of Jesus.

Worship God for giving Jesus to be your Righteousness. Remember, you are complete in Him.

Jehovah-Rohi (je-ho'-vah ro'ee)—
The Lord My Shepherd

Jehovah-Rohi is the designation of God that begins the immortal ode, Psalm 23. *Rohi* means "to feed or lead to pasture," and consequently, King David depicts God as a loving, compassionate, caring Shepherd who gently leads His flock to green pastures. No other name of Jehovah has this tender, intimate meaning. It is a name suggesting a warm, intimate relationship between God and His people, even as a shepherd to his sheep.

David could well write this psalm. He had been a shepherd as a boy, taking care of the flocks of his father Jesse, and he also had known firsthand the gentle shepherding of God in his life. He could look back to the times when Saul had chased him, hoping to take his life; times when wars arose with neighboring nations; times of sin and deep sorrow in his own household. Through it all, even the valley of the shadow of death, his testimony was,

I will fear no evil;
For You are with me;
Your rod and Your staff they comfort me.
You prepare a table before me in the presence of my enemies;
You anoint my head with oil;
My cup runs over.
Surely goodness and mercy shall follow me
All the days of my life;
And I will dwell in the House of the LORD
Forever (Ps. 23:4–6).

The picture of God as a shepherd was one David used numerous times throughout the psalms, for it depicted a close *relationship* between God and His people. Even to this day a shepherd lives day and night with his sheep. By day, he leads them to the best available grazing land with tender grass. He calls each one by name, and they respond to his voice alone. He comforts them when they are fearful or weary. He protects them from thieves and wild animals. He searches for them if they go astray. When they fall down, or through their own ignorance or belligerence harm themselves, he is there to pick them up and mend their broken bones. At night, after making sure all sheep are accounted for in the sheep cote, the good shepherd lies down across the doorway, willing to give his life, if necessary, to protect his sheep.

What a beautiful picture of Jehovah-Rohi! He offers you His hand of strength, comfort, and guidance through the snares, temptations, and pitfalls of this life. He is there to comfort your fears and restore your soul when you are so discouraged you can't go any farther. He knows you and calls you by name. He seeks you when you go astray. He pours healing ointment into your wounds and sets all bones broken in your rebellious escapades, making your "crooked places" straight. He has unselfishly given His life for you that through His death and resurrection He could destroy the works of the thief who has come to "steal, kill, and destroy" everything precious to you. And He will lead you through the valley of the shadow of death, fearing no evil, and into His Father's house where you will dwell with Him forever.

It is Jehovah-Rohi who is spoken of in Ezekiel 34:11–16:

For thus says the LORD God: "Indeed I Myself will search for My sheep and seek them out. . . . [I will deliver them.] . . . I will feed them in good pasture. . . . I will make them lie down. . . . I will seek what was lost and bring back what was driven away, bind up the broken and strengthen what was sick."

Worship Him for who He is, your Shepherd. You are complete in Him.

Jehovah-Shammah (je-ho'-vah sham'-mah)— The Lord Who Is There

Israel was different from the other nations surrounding her. God lived in her midst, and He was holy. His people, too, were to be holy, like Him. This was in striking contrast to the heathen nations round-about, which worshiped idols and did abominations. As long as the Israelites walked in a covenant of holiness, God promised to be their God and to be present among them.

His presence was with them from their beginning as a nation. Moses declared, "If Your Presence does not go with us, do not bring us up from here. For how then will it be known that Your people and I have found grace in Your sight, except *You go with us*? So we shall be separate, Your people and I, from all the people who are upon the face of the earth" (Ex. 33:15–16, emphasis added).

His presence and glory were seen first in the tent Moses had made for Him and later in the magnificent temple King Solomon built. But then the downfall of Israel began. She once again began to worship other gods. She was no longer faithful to the Holy One of Israel. God withdrew His glorious presence, and she was destroyed by her enemies, her choicest people carried off into slavery.

At this point Ezekiel had a vision of a time to come. In it he saw a beautiful, heavenly city where the glory of God dwelled: "And the name of the city from that day shall be: THE LORD IS THERE [Jehovah-Shammah]" (Ezek. 48:35).

But that time was not yet. So once again, God showed mercy to a pitiful, regathered Israel still in bondage, this time to the Romans. He sent Jesus, Emmanuel, GOD WITH US, to save His people from their sins. He was the temple, and in Him was the Holy Presence. Once again Jehovah-Shammah lived among men.

After Jesus died, rose again, and ascended back to heaven, He sent the presence back in the person of the Holy Spirit. Now *Jehovah-Shammah lives in each believer. His presence lives in your temple.* First Corinthians 3:16 asks, "Do you not know that you are the temple of God and that the Spirit of God dwells in you?"

Finally, in the new heaven and new earth that Ezekiel saw, God is preparing a place for those who love Him: "The tabernacle of God is with men, and He will dwell with them, and they shall be His people. God Himself will be with them and be their God" (Rev. 21:3).

Over and over throughout the Scriptures God admonishes, "Fear not, for I AM WITH YOU." Hebrews 13:5 promises, "For He Himself has said, *'I will never leave you nor forsake you.'* " He is the Lord who is *present*. He is not out of earshot. He has not gone on a vacation. He did not leave the office and forget to give you a phone number where He can be reached. His beeper is not turned off. His ears are ever open to your cries, for *He is there* with you. You are not alone. You never again have to face your days and nights, your crises or victories, by yourself. *He is always there.*

Worship Him for who He is. You are complete in Him.

Who Are You?

Melinda is a classic example of the woman who has no root in herself. She and I became acquainted when our sons were in first grade together. She was in a desperate situation; her husband was leaving her for another woman, but Melinda could never grasp what had happened to make him do such a thing. As we talked together, she revealed that as a child she had been reared to feel worthless. A "surprise," only child born to wealthy older parents, she was never allowed to do anything for herself. She never even learned to make her own bed and was always told what a failure she was. Consequently, when she married, her self-esteem was so nonexistent and her ignorance in matters pertaining to loving a husband and guiding a home so great that her husband threw up his hands in disgust and found someone else to take care of him. Melinda could not cook and would not dare to try because she might fail. Her house was a pigsty. She was a highly intelligent woman but had nothing to show for it except failure because she had no understanding of who she was or what she was good for. That is tragic enough, but she has three children who are replicas of herself. Her daughter has gone from one broken relationship to another; her elder son is a perpetual student who can never discover what he really wants to do with his life; her younger son, who has a brilliant IQ, is strung out on drugs and alcohol.

She blames her past for her problems, but when she was offered a way through her wilderness she chose to stay where she was because it was comfortable, it was "known." Early in our friendship, Melinda had received the Lord "with joy" and, yet because she had no root in herself, endured only for a while. I encouraged her to continue in the

Lord, to let Him help her put down roots and discover who she really was. But she couldn't seem to manage it. Twelve years now down the road, she has finished a business course and is (sometimes) able to support herself and her children. Her "outside" looks somewhat more "together," but inside she is still a lost, frightened little girl who still wonders why she was ever born and what she's good for.

Another friend was conceived out of wedlock. Ever since she discovered the circumstances surrounding her birth, she has had a deep resentment for her father and mother and has secretly blamed them for her lack of self-worth and her identity problems. She believes she was a "mistake." Consequently, she believes that God could not have a plan for her life because, in her way of thinking, she was never supposed to have been born. Therefore, she is simply drifting through life, never assuming responsibility, always dependent upon others to take care of her.

God knew what He was doing when He breathed into you the breath of life. He is the great Redeemer who redeems your life from destruction. Your parents may think you were a mistake, and you may agree with them, but GOD DOESN'T unless you reject His life and plan for you. Listen to Psalm 139:

> [O Lord,] You formed my inward parts;
> You covered me in my mother's womb.
> I will praise You, for I am fearfully and wonderfully made;
> Marvelous are Your works,
> And that my soul knows very well.
> My bones were not hidden from You,
> When I was made in secret,
> And skillfully wrought. . . .
> Your eyes saw my substance, being yet unformed.
> And in Your book they all were written,
> The days fashioned for me. . . .
> How precious also are Your thoughts to me, O God!
> How great is the sum of them!
> If I should count them, they would be more in number
>   than the sand;
> When I awake, I am still with You (vv. 13–18).

You are accepted in Jesus, the Beloved (see Eph. 1:6), and you and your children are good for "signs and wonders" (Isa. 8:18). Don't ever doubt it again!

But what are you doing with the gift of life you have received? Are you blaming your problems on someone else? Are you willing to stop looking at your failures and disappointments and begin to find your identity in Him? Are you willing to develop a prayer life? Are you willing to simply choose to believe what God has to say about you, to see yourself through His eyes instead of your own?

The old way you viewed yourself has worked death in you, but the way God sees you, "in Christ," is life-imparting. First Corinthians 15:22 says, "For as in Adam [your old nature] all die, even so in Christ all shall be made alive."

June Hunt writes in *Seeing Yourself Through God's Eyes*, "How extraordinary—every child of God genuinely has a new worth, a new destination, and a new identity!" Then she lists the following helpful Scriptures:

YOUR NEW LIFE IN CHRIST

For as in Adam all die, so in Christ all will be made alive (1 Corinthians 15:22)

For as in Adam all die		So in Christ all will be made alive	
IN ADAM		**IN CHRIST**	
Old creature	*2 Cor. 5:17*	New creature	*2 Cor. 5:17*
Unrepentant heart	*Romans 2:5*	New heart	*Ezekiel 36:26*
Slave to sin	*Romans 6:6*	Free from sin	*Romans 6:7*
Death	*Romans 6:23*	Life	*Romans 6:22*
Powerless	*Romans 5:6*	Strength	*Phil. 4:13*
Enemies of God	*Romans 5:10*	Reconciled to God	*Romans 5:10*
Condemned	*Romans 5:6*	No condemnation	*Romans 8:1*
Slave	*Gal. 3:7*	Son	*Gal. 3:7*
Slave to impurity	*Romans 6:19*	Slave to righteousness	*Romans 6:19*
Poverty	*2 Cor. 8:9*	Riches	*2 Cor. 8:9*
Accused	*Col. 1:22*	Blameless	*Col. 1:22*
Under law	*Romans 6:14*	Under grace	*Romans 6:14*
Under judgment	*Romans 5:16*	Justified	*Romans 5:16*
Under a curse	*Gal. 3:13*	Redeemed from curse	*Gal. 3:13*
Under wrath	*Eph. 5:16*	Free from wrath	*Romans 5:9*
In darkness	*Eph. 5:8*	In the light	*Eph. 5:8*

In Christ you are made alive. Old things are passed away; behold, all things are become new (see 2 Cor. 5:17). You can experience for yourself the abundance of life that Jesus died to give you. It is available to you, not just a select few.

A. W. Tozer offered some practical advice along these lines:

> Retire from the world each day to some private spot, even if it be only the bedroom (for a while I retreated to the furnace room for want of a better place). Stay in the secret place till the surrounding noises begin to fade out of your heart and a sense of God's presence envelops you. Deliberately tune out the unpleasant sounds and come out of your closest determined not to hear them. Listen for the inward Voice till you learn to recognize it. Stop trying to compete with others. Give yourself to God and then *be what and who you are* [emphasis added] without regard to what others think. . . . Learn to pray inwardly every moment. After a while you can do this even while you work. Practice candor, childlike honesty, humility. Pray for a single eye. . . . Gaze on Christ with the eyes of your soul. Practice spiritual concentration.
>
> All the above is contingent upon a right relation to God through Christ and daily meditation of the Scriptures. Lacking these, nothing will help us; granted these, the discipline recommended will go far to neutralize the evil effects of externalism and to make us acquainted with God and our own souls.

Remember, only as you know who God is and who you are in Him can you really know who you are and what you're good for.

"For I know the plans I have for you," declares the Lord, "plans to prosper you and not to harm you, plans to give you hope and a future" (Jer. 29:11 NIV).

You are complete in Him.

The Power of Praise

When I became pregnant, I did so with a vengeance: I bore three children in three and one-half years. During this time, I rode the bus 140 miles round-trip three times a week to complete my master's degree in voice. My precious mother and daddy lived with us during those years, cooking wonderful meals and ministering to our babies. Prayer was the last thing on my mind. Top priority was *survival*. I was so exhausted that I went through my days like a zombie. If I sat down for a moment, I immediately fell asleep. I remember many occasions that I would sit down to nurse Joy Elizabeth and would awaken forty-five minutes later with her sound asleep upside down under my arm. It was the grace of God that she lived to be weaned!

I had not yet received revelation concerning the Lord's Prayer and did not know that God, in His merciful understanding of mothers with small children, had given it to us in several segments that did not have to be prayed all in one sitting. It can be prayed throughout the day, woven lovingly around the multitude of interruptions that undoubtedly will come in a houseful of toddlers.

At that time what I needed more than anything else was strength. I was desperate to have enough strength just to make it through the day. I would awaken in the mornings dreading my day, strategizing the first available opportunity to catch a brief nap. And then the word of the Lord came into my heart. Each day I would hear it speaking to me, "The joy of the Lord is your strength." Over and over, throughout the day, for weeks I continued to hear, "My joy is your strength." Sometimes it takes me a while to catch on, but because I was so desperate, I finally started taking it to heart. God was speaking to me! Trying to get my attention. Trying to send aid my way. So I made a conscious choice: I decided to praise God in my circumstances, not to wait until they changed; that would take years! I began to praise Him right where I was, doing laundry, washing dishes, cleaning up spills, wiping noses and tears, playing chase and tickle, typing Larry's term papers, memorizing music.

I determined *every day,* a conscious choice, to put His praise in my mouth. To speak blessing instead of cursing; to be sweet instead of cranky; to be merciful instead of mean. When I had a basketful of shirts to iron, I learned to thank God for the husband who wore them; when I continued to wash a never-ending stream of dirty cups and glasses, I thanked God for whole, thirsty children.

It was the hardest exercise that I had ever done in my life. Some days I would be thanking God with my mouth and crying tears of exhaustion from my eyes, but I was determined to put myself in a position to be a recipient of *His* strength, for mine had long since run out. Anyone who ever finds herself in this posture is truly offering a "sacrifice of praise." It was a sacrifice. My flesh was screaming; my mind was distracted. But I was determined to keep my mouth on His praise, knowing the certainty of His promise:

> Whoever offers praise glorifies Me;
> And to him who orders his conduct aright
> I will show the salvation of God (Ps. 50:23).

"Just as antagonism, hostility, and cursing against God exercises and strengthens all that is most abominable, diabolical, and base in the human spirit," writes Dr. Paul E. Billheimer in *Destined for the Throne,* "so worship and praise of the infinitely lovely God exercises, reinforces, and strengthens all that is most sublime, transcendent, and divine in the inner being. Thus as one worships and praises, he is continually transformed step by step, from glory to glory, into the image of the infinitely happy God."

Even so, He who inhabits the praises of His people began to supernaturally manifest His joy in my life. I would awaken happy, even though I had only two to three hours of uninterrupted sleep the night before. I felt better physically, and my strength lasted longer during the day. As my days were, so was my strength (see Deut. 33:25). Although I did not understand doctrinally at the time what I was doing, I was beginning to worship Him for who He is, the strength of my life, the lifter of my head. I was learning the first part of the Lord's Prayer.

But the most valuable lesson I learned was that praise decentralizes self. Billheimer said,

> The worship and praise of God demands a shift of center from self to God. One cannot praise without relinquishing occupation with self. When praise becomes a way of life, the infinitely lovely God becomes the center of worship rather than the bankrupt self. Thus the personality becomes properly integrated. . . . This results in mental wholeness. Praise produces forgetfulness of self—and forgetfulness of self is health.

Is your identity built on anything other than the life of Christ, which is being formed in you? If so, you are standing on shifting sand, an uncertain foundation. Look unto Jesus, your Author and Finisher. When you awaken morning by morning let Him, your sympathetic High Priest, take you by the hand and lead you into the presence of God. When you are too weary, too confused, too distracted, too unconcerned to seek God on your own motivation, cry out to Jesus to lead you in. He will assist you as together you cry, "*Our* Father. . . ." Then the Father will joyfully receive you, for behold, His Son is interceding on your behalf and has made entrance for you through His own blood. Enter confidently, with full assurance of heart that you are accepted in the Beloved; that you can come as a tender little child into the warmth and protective nurture of your loving heavenly Father; that you have a place with Him not only in heaven but also in His heart. Oh, but once there, the majesty and glory of His presence, the revelation of His matchless, unselfish love, will cause you to forget yourself. You will see Him alone. And as you behold Him, praising and worshiping Him for who He is, a miracle will occur. You will be changed from faith to faith, from glory to glory. You will look less and less like your old self and more and more like Jesus. You will no longer be desperate to have an identity; you will be desperate only for more of Him. He alone is your life.

Now, without trepidation, boldly enter His gates with thanksgiving and His courts with praise. In unison with Jesus joyfully cry, "Our Father in heaven, hallowed be Your name."

8 Desperate to Be in Control

"Your kingdom come. Your will be done on earth as it is in heaven."

The joy of life and the perfection of human nature is an absolutely submitted will.

—Alexander Maclaren

I delight to do Your will, O my God.

Psalm 40:8

The battlefield of the will is strewn with the carnage of lives desperate for control: control of their own destinies and control of other people. These manipulators of power, wealth, and things are believers in the adage, "The one who dies with the most toys wins!" In our daily newspapers we see evidence of individuals desperate for control, such as the Texas woman who wanted so desperately for her daughter to become a cheerleader that she attempted to hire a hit man to kill the mother of her daughter's competitor. On an international scale we see men like Adolf Hitler and, more recently, Saddam Hussein who for their own aggrandizement seek to control whole nations and because of their insatiable egos destroy the inalienable rights of multitudes of people. Among our own friends and families we observe firsthand the destruction of the home as men and women alike proudly sing the song, "I Did It My Way," taking matters into their own hands and literally tearing their homes and the lives of the members involved into pieces.

The human will is a powerful force, which in certain instances has even battled death and conquered it for a season. But a will whose center is "self" is a will out of control, a will headed for destruction.

According to A. W. Pink, "If we conduct ourselves contrary to the revealed will of God we shall certainly suffer for it both in soul and in body, that if we follow a course of self-pleasing we shall deprive ourselves of those spiritual and temporal blessings which the Word of God promises to those whose lives are ordered by its precepts."

A prime scriptural example of one who followed "a course of self-pleasing" was Jezebel, the queen of Israel (see 1 Kings 16:29—2 Kings 9:37). Her husband, Ahab, was a weak-willed man, so Jezebel exerted tremendous influence on him. She was a treacherous woman and idolator, who manipulated the people of Israel into forsaking the living God. She killed the innocent to gain their possessions and pursued the man of God, Elijah, to take his life because he dared to oppose her. She lived violently and died violently. Her own eunuchs threw her out the window, and she was dashed on the pavement below and eaten by wild dogs. She should be the contemplation for all women who want to "do it their way."

In striking contrast is the young woman Mary, a virgin, to whom an angel appeared and announced the startling news that she would bear a son. She asked only one question: "How can these things be since I haven't had sexual relations with a man?" The angel's reply is the answer to our battle of the will: "The Holy Spirit will come upon you." Her response was the epitome of a surrendered will: "Let it be to me according to your word" (Luke 1:35, 38). For two thousand years people have indeed called her "blessed," just as she prophesied.

Quite a striking contrast, don't you think? Jezebel, tall, regal, queenly, perhaps outwardly beautiful, but inwardly, full of malicious intent and avarice; and Mary, simple, humble, perhaps not pretty, maybe even plain outwardly, but beautiful within, with a meek and quiet spirit, which is of great price in the sight of God. These two women serve as a constant reminder of the power of the will and the resulting outcome of the choices we make.

Three Methods of Control

There are three methods of control regarding the will.

First is the world's control. This form of control is the result of "outside" control, which forces you to succumb to its pressures. You are controlled by others, whether they be flesh and blood, demonic spirits, or things. At any rate, your will is no longer your own but has become enslaved to another.

Examples are evident everywhere: the Tiananmen Square massacre in Beijing, China, where a government is so obsessed with controlling the people that would-be reformers were killed as they sought to obtain, through peaceful means, expanded freedoms; crack cocaine addicts who are so enslaved to tiny white crystals that they will sell their bodies and souls just to get enough money to buy another fix; young people currently on death row who, while high on drugs and performing satanic rituals at the insistence of "voices," murdered their parents.

Second is "self"-control. This is not to be confused with the fruit borne by the Holy Spirit in the life of yielded Christians. This control is characterized by the inability to submit your will to another; the compulsion is to always "be in charge." "Self"-control is evidenced by the individual's insistence on being in charge of her life. "Self" is enthroned, and the philosophy "my way is the best way" reigns supreme. The fallacy of this thinking is in the belief that if you can control your life and the lives of others, you are insulated from being victimized by life. But life is full of the unexpected, much of which we have little control over. A person who lives in this manner will eventually burn out, blow up, or quit. It's just too hard, too impossible, and too big a "drag." I learned firsthand about this dead-end street while in college.

Having just escaped a couple of friendships in which I felt manipulated and victimized, I decided, "It's time to wise up. No more are you going to let people treat you this way. From now on, you are going to call the shots." A little dose of this leads to wisdom; an excess of it excludes the will of God. Unfortunately, I was deceived by the latter and set about to work hard, to achieve much, but always on *my* terms, always to *my* advantage. Two years later, I collapsed one afternoon on my bed, exhausted from the responsibility of running my own life my own way. As I closed my eyes hoping for blessed rest, I had instead a disconcerting vision. All the "wonderful" things I had done the past two years—all in the name of the Lord, all trying to be a "good," if misguided, Christian—all passed before me and then caught fire, burning up as wood, hay, and stubble. I was so shaken, I immediately reached for my Bible. It fell open (coincidentally, I'm sure) to John 10:10: "I have come that [you] may have life, and that [you] may have it more abundantly." In response I declared disgustedly, "Somebody's wrong!" And then I heard a still, small voice quietly reply, "Well, it's not ME!" Dumbfounded, I fearfully looked around my room, thinking someone must have entered without my knowledge. But when I realized no one else was there—that is, no one I could *see!*—I bolted in terror off the bed and out the door.

In *The Pursuit of God,* A. W. Tozer wrote, "It would seem that there is within each of us an enemy which we tolerate at our peril. Jesus called it 'life' and 'self,' or as we would say, the *self-life*."

As Jesus said, "If anyone desires to come after Me, let him deny himself, and take up his cross, and follow Me. For whoever desires to save his life will lose it, but whoever loses his life for My sake will find it" (Matt. 16:24–25).

I had been seeking to preserve my own life, not denying myself but instead pleasing myself. And I had a mouthful of ashes to prove it.

Third is control by the Holy Spirit. Ephesians 5:18 admonishes, "Be filled with the Spirit," that is, be continuously controlled by the Holy Spirit of God. He knows the higher plans and purposes of God concerning your life, and He knows the plans of the enemy to thwart the accomplishing of those purposes. Lean completely on Him, the One who goes alongside and aids you. Do not fear. He has plans of good and not evil for you.

The Kingdom of God

When later I read in Matthew 5:3, "Blessed are the poor in spirit, for theirs is the kingdom of heaven," I realized I was certainly a candidate for the kingdom, for my life was bereft of all I had held in esteem. I was like a freight train on a downhill run, totally out of control, without an engineer at the throttle.

Not knowing what else to do at this point, since no one else was dictating my life and I had given up on my own abilities to manage it, and since I knew absolutely zero about this new life in the kingdom of God, I searched the Scriptures for answers. I discovered verses such as John 18:36, "My kingdom is not of this world"; Romans 14:17, "The kingdom of God is not eating and drinking, but righteousness and peace and joy in the Holy Spirit"; and finally, 1 Corinthians 4:20, "For the kingdom of God is not in word but in power." It sounded wonderful! I wanted desperately to live in this kingdom, to experience the benefits of this life, to fully comprehend what the Scripture meant when it said, "Where the Spirit of the Lord is, there is liberty" (2 Cor. 3:17).

Emotions Versus the Will

Up until this time my life as a Christian had been governed by my emotions. Being experientially ignorant of the benefits of kingdom life, I had believed the lie popular during my teenage years—the moodier you were, the more creative and intellectual you were esteemed to be. Appealing to the pride of life, this deception carried over into my spiritual walk, where my faith was a slave to my emotions. Through a divine encounter with Hannah Whitall Smith's *The Christian's Secret of a Happy Life,* I was forever changed. She wrote,

> Life is not to be lived in the emotions at all, but in the will. . . . It is sometimes thought that the emotions are the governing power in our nature. But I think we all of us know, as a matter of practical experience, that there is something within us, behind our emotions and behind our wishes, an independent self, that, after all, decides everything and controls everything. Our emotions belong to us, and are suffered and enjoyed by us, but they are not ourselves; and if God is to take possession of us, it must be into this central will or personality that He enters. If, then, He is reigning there by *the power of His Spirit* [emphasis added], all the rest of our nature must come under His sway; and as the will is, so is the man.

Every emotion and every thought can be brought into captivity to the power of the Spirit of God, who has taken possession of the will thus put in His hands. The Holy Spirit enables us to crown Jesus Lord of all the kingdoms of our hearts. He is the trusted friend and comforter whom Jesus promised would come upon us to guide us into all truth. In the past, your life was under the control of sin and self, which worked death in you. But now, the Holy Spirit will take the will thus yielded to Him and work mightily in you, both to will and to do His good pleasure.

The will thus yielded to Him is not a weak, insipid, spineless wonder; the one thus yielded is not left without any will at all. On the contrary, as Hannah Whitall Smith penned it: "We are simply to substitute for our foolish, misdirected wills of ignorance and immaturity the higher, divine, mature will of God."

Remember Isaiah 55:6–9:

> Seek the LORD while He may be found,
> Call upon Him while He is near.
> Let the wicked forsake his way,
> And the unrighteous man his thoughts;
> Let him return to the LORD,
> And He will have mercy on him;
> And to our God,

For he will abundantly pardon.
"For My thoughts are not your thoughts,
Nor are your ways My ways," says
the LORD.
"For as the heavens are higher than the earth,
So are My ways higher than your ways,
And My thoughts than your thoughts."

When You Pray, Say . . .

The statements, "Your kingdom come," and "Your will be done," actually are expressed in the language as, my husband has often said, a man emphatically putting his foot down, demanding, "COME Your kingdom. BE DONE Your will." This is no pitiful "If it be Your will" kind of praying. It is a declaration of faith, an affirmation that God indeed has a kingdom and a will—and that you want nothing less than His perfect will to be effectuated in your life.

When our children were very small, I began to pray this declaration with them each day: "COME *Your* kingdom. BE DONE *Your* will in John, Jo Anna, and Joy. Not the will of their flesh or someone else; not the will of any devil. Only *Your* will be done in them today!" The fruit of this kind of praying has been evidenced throughout the years. At each turning point in our life as a family, the children would say to Larry and me, "Dad and Mom, you discern what God's will is, and we'll all do it." They have experienced firsthand the blessedness, peace, and joy of living life in the will of God. Anything less would be a travesty.

When praying over your priorities, begin first with yourself. If you are not in right standing before God, how can you pray effectively for anyone else? Command, "COME kingdom of God in me—nothing short of righteousness, peace, and joy to exude from me today. Fill me with your Holy Spirit so that the fruit of the Spirit will be manifest *in* me and the power of God be released *through* me."

Everything in the universe moves in precise divine order, from atoms to planets, everything, that is, except *people*. We insist on charting our own course even when we have no idea where we're going. We prefer our way to His way, our disorder for His divine order. But when the child of God fully submits her will and emotions to the Holy Spirit, rising daily and declaring, "Not my will but Yours be done today! COME kingdom of God! BE DONE will of God!" then supernaturally God begins to realign her life to His pleasing. Divine order will begin to be established in her priorities, in her home, in her relationships, in every area of life she is willing to submit to the scrutiny of the Holy Spirit.

When Larry and I first married, we had not yet received revelation concerning this part of the Lord's Prayer, yet we did understand that everything in the universe operated according to divine plan. We so desired to be in the very center of the will of God for our lives that we began to agree together with God that He would set us in order. Oh, boy! Little did I realize the struggle I was about to experience. Growing up a strong-willed only child, believing that anything a man could do I could do better, and perceiving marriage to be a 50–150 split in my favor, not the 200 percent actually required of each partner, I was in for some *serious* restructuring. As Larry and I asked God to bring our home into divine order, the Holy Spirit began to turn up the heat, making the ugly impurities rise to the surface. My bossy, controlling, "I'm always right!" attitude became a humiliation. Without fail, every time we paused at a stop sign or traffic light, not knowing which way to go—invariably whatever directions came out of my mouth—it was precisely reverse! Day after day this happened, until finally whenever Larry would ask, "Which way should we turn?" he did the exact opposite of *whatever* I replied, knowing of a certainty that it would be the correct decision.

We can laugh about it now (just a little), but then, oh, how I cried! I had always been in control of my life. Now I was married to *this man,* and suddenly every decision I made, made me look like a *fool*. I was utterly humiliated but gradually, through brokenness, was coming into divine order.

When you begin to declare, "COME Your kingdom! BE DONE Your will!" expect it to happen! Your flesh may run around screaming at you, things may get worse before they get better, but remember you are God's workmanship, created unto good works. He loves you too much to leave you the way you are! If you persevere and don't give up, righteousness, peace, and joy in the Holy Spirit will be actualized as your daily portion, and your life will begin to flow in God's greater eternal purpose for you. Hang in there! It's worth it!

E. M. Bounds wrote,

> Our secret will determines our character and controls our conduct. Our will, therefore, plays an important part in all

successful praying. There can be no rich, true praying when the will is not wholly and fully surrendered to God. This unswerving loyalty to God is an utterly indispensable condition of the best, truest, and most effective praying. We have simply *got* to "trust and obey. *There's no other way,* to be happy in Jesus—but to trust and *obey*!"

Regardless of how much it pained me, I determined to stay committed to this declaration of faith. Once again, I threw myself upon the mercy of God, resolving to live this way for the duration, and settled down to simply trust and obey.

Praying the Word

"Prayer is not a mere form of words," said Bounds.

It is not just calling upon a name. Prayer is *obedience.* . . . Our Lord plainly taught: "Not everyone which saith unto Me, Lord, Lord, shall enter the kingdom of heaven; but *he that doeth the will of My Father* which is in heaven. Many will say unto Me in that day, Lord, Lord, have we not prophesied in Thy name? and in Thy name have cast out evils? and in Thy name done many wonderful works? And then will I profess unto them, I never knew you: depart from Me, ye that worketh iniquity" (Matt. 7:21–23).

Being persuaded that the will of God was a much higher and safer path in which to walk than my own stumbling, chuckhole-filled road, and being convinced that it was absolutely essential to kingdom life, I set out to focus more specifically on just *what was the will of God.* I remember saying many times, "If I just knew *what* was the will of God, I'd do it!"

Bounds asked this same question:

How are we to know what God's will is? The answer is by studying His Word, by hiding it in our hearts, and by letting the Word dwell in us richly. "The entrance of Thy words, giveth light" (Ps. 119:130).

To know God's will in prayer, we must be filled with God's Spirit, who makes intercession for the saints according to the will of God. *To be filled with God's Spirit, and to be filled with God's Word, is to know God's will.* It is to be put in such a frame of mind and state of heart that it will enable us to read and correctly interpret the purposes of the infinite. Such filling of the heart with the Word and the Spirit gives us an insight into the will of the Father. It enables us to rightly discern His will and puts a disposition of mind and heart within us to make it the guide and compass of our lives.

But I want to encourage you to know God's will in prayer by taking it one step further. Not only should you be filled with the Spirit and the Word to rightly discern the will of God and pray effectively, but you can begin to move in a more *powerful* realm of prayer by actually *praying the Word*.

God honors His Word above His name. His Word is His revealed will. Instead of bemoaning the fact that you do not know all the revealed will of God concerning whatever situation you are currently facing, apply a specific Scripture to what you *know* to be His will.

Madame Guyon wrote in her highly esteemed little book *Experiencing God Through Prayer,* "St. Augustine once blamed himself for all the lost time trying to find God's will when, from the very beginning, he could have done so by this manner of *praying the Word*."

It was from my precious friend and colaborer in prayer and spiritual warfare, Kathy Casto, that I learned this powerful secret of praying the Word. In her wonderfully practical booklet *How to Pray for Your Loved Ones,* she observes,

> The word of God is truth and what it says . . . is God's will for your life. Do not be deceived by the circumstances you face today. They are only a smokescreen to discourage you and keep you from praying. Don't speak negative words over your situation. This only distorts your vision and keeps your eyes focused on the *problem* instead of the *promise*—on what "appears to be" rather than truth, which is the word of God.
>
> When you pray the word it will build your faith for "faith cometh by hearing, and hearing by the word of God" (Rom. 10:17). You pray the word. You hear the word. Your faith increases. Morning by morning your faith grows stronger until you no longer see the situation as it appears momentarily, but you see it through the eyes of the Spirit—confident that God is working in your behalf. It is only a matter of time before you receive the answer.

Then Kathy proceeds to list specific Scriptures that God has quickened to her over the years for particular needs in her life. Declaring,

"COME Your kingdom; BE DONE Your will in me today," she prays verses over herself such as:

> Open my ears to hear what your Spirit is saying for "Ears that hear and eyes that see—the LORD has made them both" (Prov. 20:12 NIV).

> Set a guard . . . over my mouth;
> Keep watch over the door of my lips (Ps. 141:3).

> Let the words of my mouth and the meditation of my heart
> Be acceptable in Your sight,
> O LORD, my strength and my Redeemer (Ps. 19:14).

> Direct my steps by Your word (Ps. 119:133).

> Teach us to number our days,
> That we may gain a heart of wisdom (Ps. 90:12)

Over her husband she declares the will of God with such verses as:

> The Spirit of the LORD shall rest upon Him,
> The Spirit of wisdom and understanding,
> The Spirit of counsel and might,
> The Spirit of knowledge and of the fear of the LORD.
> His delight is in the fear of the LORD (Isa. 11:2–3).

> Beloved, I pray that you may prosper in all things and be in health, just as your soul prospers (3 John 2).

> The king's heart is in the hand of the LORD,
> Like the rivers of water, He turns it wherever He wishes
> (Prov. 21:1).

Over her children she personalizes verses such as:

> Father, let (children's names) pay attention to what I say and listen closely to my words. Do not let them out of their sight, help them to keep them within their hearts; for they are life to those who find them and health to their flesh. Above all else, help them to guard the heart, for it is the wellspring of life (Prov. 4:20–23).

> May they apply their hearts to instruction and their ears to words of knowledge (Prov. 23:12).

> And just as Jesus grew in wisdom and stature and in favor with God and men, let it be so for my children (Luke 2:52).

Through Kathy's example, I and a multitude of other women have become more equipped to do the will of God.

In circumstances wherein the solution is not so easily defined, wait upon the Holy Spirit. Allow Him to fill your heart and mind and direct you in the Word of God. Presently He will fit the "sword" in your hand, a phrase, a passage, a *living* word (just as Jesus had in the wilderness when withstanding the devil), which will be precisely the declaration necessary for His kingdom to come and His will to be done in your situation.

Some may argue, "This sounds like spiritual witchcraft where you are manipulating God with His Word to do *your* will."

Do you think God is so ignorant as to fall prey to manipulation? Those who would argue in this way have missed the point entirely. If you have yielded your will to God, asked the Holy Spirit to come and fill you, to guide you in the Word of God so that you can be more like Jesus, do you think for a moment that anything short of *His will* will be accomplished?

Come on! Get off the excuses, and just go *do* it. Exercise the "sword of the Spirit, which is the word of God" (Eph. 6:17), and see how the mountains begin to move in your life. Experience the joy that being a colaborer with God brings to your heart. Encounter the Holy Spirit for yourself, and witness how real He is, how powerfully He can work in your behalf.

In *The Father Heart of God,* Floyd McClung, Jr., writes,

> When Jesus knelt alone to talk with the Father on that fateful night in the Garden of Gethsemane, His heart was heavy. He faced the ultimate trial—death. His Father had asked a hard thing of Him, but He was not forced to act against His will. He accepted His Father's plan because He knew and trusted Him.
>
> Christ said, "Not my will but Thine be done." Because He knew God's heart, He obeyed Him unconditionally. It was not a forced response to an overbearing Father, but a trusting response to known love.

How will you respond to God's revelation of His love for you? Will you continue to demand control of the reins of your life? Will you seek to manipulate others or allow others to manipulate you? Will you allow yourself to be subjected to the tyranny of your emotions or to be set free by the choice of your will?

As the Holy Spirit seeks to conform you into the image of Jesus, see that you do not resist Him. Let your response be one that reveals more clearly than anything else how secure you feel in His love: "I delight to do your will, O God. Not my will, but Thine be done."

9 Desperate to Be Secure

"Give us this day our daily bread."

Since then no absolute security against want can be found on earth,
it necessarily follows, that he who trusts in God is the most wise
and prudent man. Who dare deny that the promise of the living God
is an absolute security?

—*John Stevenson, from C. H. Spurgeon's* The Treasury of David

Jesus never lied to us. He never promised life on this earth was
going to be a bed of roses. Instead, He warned us, "As long as you
live in this world, you will have tribulation." He thoroughly under-
stood that the principle of sin was running rampant throughout His
creation, and either with or without our willing involvement, each of
our lives would sometimes resemble an earthquake, a tornado, or a
headlong tumble down the stairs. It would not have surprised Him
that by 1990, violence against women in America would have increased 50 percent over the previous fifteen years; that every six seconds, a woman would be raped; that every eighteen seconds, one
would be beaten; that in the Dallas/Ft. Worth Metroplex alone, one-
half of all marriages would end in divorce. The statistics on divorce
would have broken His heart but not astonished Him: in the first year
after a divorce, a woman's income decreases by 73 percent while a
man's increases by 42 percent; five years later, her income is still 30
percent less than it was during the marriage; and this is regardless of
social class and regardless of who left whom.

No, Jesus had no naive incredulity. He was intimately acquainted
with the insecurities and griefs of this life: the fickleness of public
opinion, the betrayal of those most loved and trusted, the lack of understanding from family, no home to call His own, no bed upon which
to lay His head but what was supplied to Him through the loving
benevolence of others. When the Twelve promised undying loyalty,
Jesus responded with these words of foresight:

Indeed the hour is coming, yes, has now come, that you will be scattered, each to his own, and will leave Me alone. And yet I am not alone, *because the Father is with Me*. These things I have spoken to you, that *in Me* you may have *peace. In the world* you will have *tribulation;* but be of good cheer, I have overcome the world (John 16:32–33, emphasis added).

"The Father is with Me." Can you grasp the security of that thought? The Father was with Jesus and even now is with you. The One who said He has engraved your name on His palms promised that NO ONE would be able under any circumstances to pluck you out of His hands. The same One who promised, "I will never leave you, nor forsake you," sent His Son to overcome the world for you. The promises of His Word are powerful and enduring. Jesus covenanted with us, "Heaven and earth will pass away, but *My words will by no means pass away*" (Matt. 24:35, emphasis added).

What a tremendous guarantee! Though our whole world crumble around us, everything in which we've trusted, there is something that will never be dislodged in heaven or earth—His *Word*—His promises—they are eternal, never changing, and unmistakably life rearranging!

Unfortunately, many people relegate the words of God to the same level as the words of man. In their experience they've said, "All men are liars, so I probably can't trust God either." As J. B. Phillips wrote in *Your God Is Too Small,* "The trouble with many people today is that they have not found a God big enough for modern needs. . . . Their ideas of God have remained largely static. It is obviously impossible for an adult to worship the conception of God that exists in the mind of a child of Sunday-school age, unless he is prepared to deny his own experience of life."

But to deny your own experience is not honest, and a relationship with God that is to be real and meaningful must be truthful and honest. God is truth, and in Him dwells no lie. He longs for the gap to be bridged between where *He* is and where *you* are in experience so that you might really know Him; know Him in His ability to care for you, to be a very present help in time of trouble; know Him as the tender Shepherd who constantly guards, guides, protects, and feeds His sheep; know Him as the One who is mighty to save and will, of a surety, make a way for you through the wilderness of this life.

But even as you have decided to believe God when He promised, "I will be a father to the fatherless and will put the solitary in families" (see Ps. 68:5–6): even as you believed His word concerning the power of the blood of Jesus, power to cleanse you from all unrighteousness, guilt, and shame and give you an everlasting entrance into the Father's presence; even as you believed that an eternal home is being prepared for you, and that you will never taste death but will instead pass from this life into the next; even as you have begun to look at Him, worshiping Him for who He is, and to see yourself in Him, complete; even as He has an everlasting kingdom in which He wants you to participate and a will concerning your life; even so, God desires to once again validate all of the above by moving you out of the ethereal into the realm of knowing Him in daily practicality, out of the nebulous "waters" and "fire" of poetic verse, and into the here and now. That is why it is no coincidence that at this point in the prayer, Jesus instructed, "Pray . . . give us this day our daily bread." He knew that many of us would be willing to believe in the celestial aspects of life, but without a balancing, daily practicality, we would know Him only in theory, not in actuality.

God is real, and if we are to have a relationship with Him, we must be real, too. And this is where the "rubber meets the road," where we discover if we really believe what we preach. I'm talking about *money* or, rather, the lack of it. The best way to get real—really quickly—is in the day-in, day-out reality of finances! Do you have enough money to pay the rent? Is the car going to be repossessed? Can the grocery money stretch a little farther? When *will* you be able to afford a new dress or shoes? Is college in the realm of possibility for your kids? Does God care? Where is Jehovah-Jireh?

A dear friend once said, "Needs change from time to time, but the fact of life is that when one need is met, another need presents itself. You are never without a need."

Does God care? Yes, He cares. He is concerned about your needs. As Robert Schuller notes, "God is not honored when a human creature lives in abject poverty. Poverty enslaves, demeans and humiliates individuals, stripping them of their dignity as human beings." Third John 2 says, "Beloved, I pray *that you may prosper* in all things and be in health, just as your soul prospers" (emphasis added). God wants to help you. He wants to *lift* you. That's the beauty of the gospel: its *lifting power* in every dimension of your life.

But how do you move the hand of God in the mundane but nonrelenting money pressures of life? The answer is simply through faith.

Without faith it is impossible to please Him, so faith is the starting point. Whoever comes to God must believe that He is, and that He is a *rewarder* of them who diligently seek Him (see Heb. 11:6).

"But," you object, "I have no faith. If you had been through the trouble I've experienced, you'd not have any faith either." That is in contradiction to Romans 12:3, which says that God has given to *every person* a measure of faith. That means *you* have a measure of faith, but perhaps it's on the bottom of the pile, hidden under a stack of miserable experiences, doubt, and unbelief. The only sure remedy for an injured or buried faith is to cry out to the Lord, the Author and Finisher of your faith, even as did the desperate father who sought Jesus' help to heal his son. "Lord," he cried, "I believe. Help my unbelief!" (Mark 9:24).

Romans 10:17 teaches, "So then faith comes by hearing, and hearing by the Word of God." Good news! Faith *comes*—it's on the way! But are you in a position to receive it? You will be unable to receive it when it arrives on your doorstep if you are not positioning yourself to hear the Word of God. Are you worshiping with other believers where the Bible is taught without apology? Are you searching the Scriptures daily for yourself, trusting the Holy Spirit to quicken the word of God once again to your heart and resurrect your faith? Are you shutting your ears to voices of fear, doubt, and unbelief and setting your face like a flint to seek God? If so, you are moving into a position for faith to come!

As it is written in 1 John, "This is the victory that has overcome the world—our faith" (5:4). This victory is not won without a battle, for the enemy who has come to steal, kill, and destroy all that you have is not willing to quietly acquiesce to your pleadings and make life easier on you. On the contrary, he delights in destroying everything precious to you and necessary for your financial well-being. You must resist him steadfastly in the faith, as the apostle Paul admonished, taking care to be a doer of the word, not just a hearer, thereby deceiving yourself (see James 1:22).

But as a weary friend once said to me, "I don't want a bunch of religious jargon. I just want victory over these finances! I'm so tired of the same money struggles over and over again, of everybody looking to me for the answers, as if *I'm* the Savior! I don't know how to do more than I'm already doing. I wish I had somebody who would take care of *me!*"

One woman married with that idea in mind: "When I got married,

I thought, *This man is going to take care of me.* As it turned out, he wanted me to take care of him!"

Is this your answer to the security issue in your life, too? If so, you will periodically face the fears of the "what if's": "What if my husband leaves me?" "What if we lose our business?" "What if . . . what if . . . what if . . ."

As Alice Slaikeu Lawhead remarked in *The Lie,* "It's an act of faith to turn those 'what if's' into 'even if.' Even if my husband leaves me, even if my daughter is on drugs, even if I lose my job . . . God will love me and I will survive."

John Stevenson said it with great clarity,

> He who relies on the promise of God for the supply of his temporal wants, possesses an infinitely greater security than the individual who confides in his accumulated wealth. . . . Since then no absolute security against want can be found on earth, it necessarily follows, that he who trusts in God is the most wise and prudent man. Who dare deny that the promise of the living God is an absolute security?

In all of this troubled earth, there is *no* lasting security apart from the promises of a living, loving God. He alone knows what lies ahead. He alone knows where and when your "door of hope" will open. He alone is the unshakable rock, Jehovah-Jireh, your Provider, who knows what you have need of before you ask, whose storehouses are full of ample provision.

The reality of Psalm 23:1 is strong: "The LORD is my shepherd; I shall not want." Matthew Henry wrote in his *Commentary,* "Let not those fear starving that are at God's finding, and have Him for their Feeder. More is implied than is expressed; not only, *I shall not want,* but 'I shall be supplied with whatever I need; and if I have not everything I desire, I may conclude it is either not fit for me, or not good for me, or I shall have it in due time.'"

Your faith in God's promises is the means necessary to obtain your daily bread. If you are walking in obedience to the specific commands of Scripture concerning finances, you can expect, without fail, the supernatural intervention of God. He delights to show Himself strong on behalf of those who love Him and obey His Word. But what are the specific points of obedience He requires?

1. Scriptural Work Habits

"In all labor there is profit, but idle chatter leads only to poverty," asserts the proverb (14:23).

When God created the earth and everything upon it, He did so in six days; on the seventh He rested. Into this divine order He placed man and woman and gave them dominion over the Garden. Six days a week they enjoyed the fruit of their labor; it was a continual challenge and pleasure to them. The seventh they rested and fellowshiped with God, giving Him the opportunity to rejuvenate them physically, spiritually, and mentally. The same creativity God Himself possessed, He put into man and woman. Consequently, Adam had the ability to name countless multitudes of animals, and he and Eve had the knowledge necessary to tend the Garden.

God gives people the ability to work. It is the blessing of the Lord upon our lives. Just ask the person who has had that opportunity removed through disease or tragedy. But often in our pleasure-crazed society, the word *work* is a dirty word. We would rather live on a perpetual vacation. Yet the apostle Paul said that the person too lazy to work should not be able to eat, and that the person too lazy to support the family was worse than an infidel.

Diligence is a virtue promulgated in the Scripture: "Whatever your hand finds to do [whatever your occupation], do it with your might" (Eccl. 9:10). This applies not just to work you find intellectually stimulating or especially creative but in whatever endeavor you are engaged. If you will be faithful where you are, God, who is in charge of promotions (see Ps. 75:6-7), will give you more with which to be faithful. But if you are not faithful with what you now have, even it will be taken away from you (see Mark 4:25).

Mary Crowley of Home Interiors and Gifts, Inc., is a shining example of a diligent woman. Orphaned at an early age, she learned that in order to succeed you must be diligent. As a young divorced woman during the Great Depression, she suddenly found herself the sole support of herself and two small children. But instead of being lazy or feeling sorry for herself, Mary set out to find work. She didn't know that no one was hiring—she just knew that she was a hard worker, and whoever hired her was going to get the best employee he ever had! That very day she came home with a job.

As her children grew and needs became greater, Mary managed to obtain a scholarship from the Rotary Club in order to go to business college. By day she worked; at night she went to school while relatives helped with her children. Eventually, she was able to establish her own company, which reflected her Christian values, and reach her goal in life: to help women help themselves. Because of her diligence and the promotion of God, Mary Crowley did not remain obscure. In 1977 she was invited to the White House; in 1978 she was the recipient of the Horatio Alger Award. She was the first woman to ever sit on the board of directors of the Billy Graham Evangelistic Association, the Direct Sales Association, and the Dallas Chamber of Commerce.

"Do you see a [woman] diligent and skillful in [her] business? [She] will stand before kings; [she] will not stand before obscure people" (Prov. 22:29 AMPLIFIED)—Mary Crowley is the personification of this verse.

Both apostles Paul and Peter gave sound scriptural advice to employees. In Titus 2:9-10 (AMPLIFIED), Paul wrote,

> [Tell] bondservants [employees] to be submissive to their masters [employers], to be pleasing and give satisfaction in every way. [Warn them] not to talk back or contradict, nor to steal by taking things of small value, but to prove themselves truly loyal and entirely reliable and faithful throughout, so that in everything they may be an ornament and do credit to the teaching [which is from and about] God our Savior.

Peter encouraged employees to continue to work honorably even in the face of persecution:

> Servants [employees], be submissive to your masters [employers] with all (proper) respect, not only to those who are kind, considerate and reasonable but also to those who are surly—overbearing, unjust and crooked. For one is regarded favorably (is approved, acceptable and thankworthy) if, as in the sight of God, he endures the pain of unjust suffering. [After all] what kind of glory [is there in it] if when you do wrong and are punished for it you take it patiently? But if you bear patiently with suffering [which results] when you do right and that is undeserved, it is acceptable and well-pleasing to God. For even to this were you called—it is inseparable from your vocation. For Christ also suffered for you, leaving you [His personal] example, so that you should follow on in His footsteps. He was guilty of no sin; neither was deceit (guile) ever found on His lips. When He was reviled and insulted, He did not revile or offer insult

in return; [when] He was abused and suffered, He made no threats [of vengeance]; but He trusted [Himself and everything] to Him Who judges fairly (1 Pet. 2:18–23 AMPLIFIED).

If you are working under less-than-happy circumstances, don't walk in and resign in a huff. Why should you be unemployed and miss paying the rent? Proverbs 21:5 offers some wisdom: "The plans of the diligent lead surely to plenty, but those of everyone who is hasty, surely to poverty." Stay where you are, letting Christ form in you, all the while diligently searching for a "door of promotion" and keeping your ears open for a "God idea."

2. God Ideas

God gives creative ideas that become the means by which we can obtain financial blessings: "And you shall remember the LORD your God, for *it is He who gives you power to get wealth,* that He may establish His covenant which He swore to your fathers, as it is this day" (Deut. 8:18, emphasis added). God made a covenant with Abraham whereby all of his children would be blessed. We are children of Abraham because we are children of faith. Therefore, the covenant remains in effect for us. God wants to bless *you* in order *to make you a blessing.* In order to do so, He will give you creative ideas that are the power to obtain wealth.

Dr. Schuller says, "Be careful of the ideas that you allow to enter your mind—especially when the economy is in an unstable condition. God can give you inspiring ideas that turn obstacles into opportunities, problems into possibilities."

Do you recognize any of these names?

John D. Rockefeller, Sr.
J. C. Penney
J. L. Kraft
William Colgate
Mary Kay Ash
Mary Crowley

Each individual started out with little financial means but faith in a great God; each was equipped with a God idea, desiring to benefit not only his or her family but also the kingdom of God. Mary Kay Ash, like her sister-in-law and friend, Mary Crowley, wanted to lift women, to give them a means to support themselves while working in their own homes and enable them to have self-respect. She was diligent, and God gave her an idea—Mary Kay Cosmetics—which has developed into a gigantic blessing not only for her family but for multitudes of other women who have worked with her over the years.

These entrepreneurs were diligent men and women, equipped with God ideas, who desired to turn their blessing from God into a blessing for someone else, and each one also testified to being a faithful steward of *God's* money.

3. Stewardship

The most crucial point of obedience concerning financial security is in the multifaceted area of stewardship. A steward is one who manages the affairs of another. Even as Jesus taught, we will one day stand before God and give an account of the stewardship of our lives. Consequently, it would be advantageous to carefully consider the following questions:

Are you seeking to live within your means, or does the "lust of the eyes" have a heyday with your wallet and you are hard-pressed not to buy everything you see? Are you tempted to be ruled by the "pride of life" and feel it's imperative to keep up with your friends even when you cannot afford to do so? Remember the words of Jesus in Luke 12:15: "Take heed and beware of covetousness: for one's life does not consist in the abundance of the things [she] possesses." On the contrary, "godliness with contentment is great gain" (1 Tim. 6:6).

Stewardship involves wisdom for managing what you keep and obedience to the scriptural injunctions concerning *giving*. To ignore these admonitions is to forsake your mercy. When God gave commandments regarding giving, He did not do so to *reduce* you but to *increase* you. "Give, and it will be given to you," commanded Jesus. "Good measure, pressed down, shaken together, and running over will be put into your bosom. For with the same measure that you use, it will be measured back to you" (Luke 6:38). Proverbs 11:24–25 teaches the same thing:

> There is one who scatters, yet increases more;
> And there is one who withholds more than is right,
> But it leads to poverty.
> The generous soul will be made rich,
> And he who waters will also be watered himself.

There are three scriptural ways in which to give in obedience to the Word of God: alms gifts, tithes, and offerings.

Alms are usually thought of as something people gave to beggars sometime in the past, but alms are still in vogue today as far as God is concerned. The Scriptures are replete with admonitions to remember the poor; to always keep a heart that is merciful toward their plight and a hand always extended to those less fortunate than ourselves. If we sow thusly, we can expect a return blessing upon ourselves if we should ever be in similar unfortunate circumstances. Psalm 41:1 declares, "Blessed is he who considers the poor; the LORD will deliver him in time of trouble." One proverb asserts, "He who has pity on the poor lends to the LORD, and He will pay back what he has given" (19:17). And another proverb admonishes, "He who gives to the poor will not lack, but he who hides his eyes will have many curses" (28:27).

Jesus gave instruction on how to correctly give alms:

> Take heed that ye do not your alms before men, to be seen of them: otherwise ye have no reward of your Father which is in heaven. . . . But when thou doest alms, let not thy left hand know what thy right hand doeth: that thine alms may be in secret: and thy Father which seeth in secret himself shall reward thee openly (Matt. 6:1, 3–4 KJV).

Notice Jesus did not say, "*If* you give alms." He said, "*When*."

Billy Graham, in his sermon "Partners With God," says, "One of the greatest sins in America today is the fact that we are robbing God of that which rightfully belongs to Him. When we don't tithe, we shirk a just debt."

Listen to what God said in Malachi 3:8–11 (AMPLIFIED):

> Will a [woman] rob or defraud God? Yet you rob and defraud Me. But you say, In what way do we rob or defraud You? *You have withheld your tithes and offerings.*
>
> You are cursed with the curse; for you are robbing Me, even this whole nation.
>
> Bring all the tithes—the whole tenth of your income—into the storehouse, that there may be food in My house, and prove Me now by it, says the Lord of hosts, if I will not open the windows of heaven for you and pour you out a blessing, that there shall not be room enough to receive it.

> And I will rebuke the devourer for your sakes, and he shall not
> destroy the fruits of your ground; neither shall your vine drop its
> fruit before the time in the field, says the Lord of hosts.

When, as a principle of life, we first take care of God's house and interests, He promises in turn to pour blessings upon us so great that it will be hard for us to contain them. In addition, He personally will rebuke the devil on our account, giving commandment that "our stuff" is not to be "messed with," and our blessing (fruit on the vine) will not be aborted.

Another reason that God commands us to tithe is to ensure that we are never without seed to sow. God gives seed to the sower. Without seed, you have no chance for a harvest. Ask any farmer. First, the seed must be put into the ground; then at the right season, the harvest will appear. When you fail to obey God with your tithe, you are just like a farmer who eats his seed. He is foolish then to sit on his porch expectantly awaiting his harvest. It will never appear. The field was never sown!

Remember the promise: "Whatever a man sows, that will he also reap. . . . And let us not grow weary while doing good, for in due season we shall reap if we do not lose heart" (Gal. 6:7, 9).

Don Carter, Mary Crowley's son, has told of his mother's penchant for tithing: "When I was a little boy riding the bus to church here on Sundays, I used to see my mother working two jobs just to keep food on the table. She was so hardheaded, she said we were going to tithe. And at the time I thought, *We sure could use that money for other things*. I see now how God has taken that money and blessed us through it."

Billy Graham explained the difference between a tithe and an offering when he said, "Actually we are not giving when we give God one-tenth, for it belongs to Him already. This is a debt we owe. Not until we have given a tenth do we actually *begin* making an offering to the Lord."

An offering is something freely presented to God as an act of worship or devotion over and above the tithe. It cuts into *your* portion; it is a sacrifice; it costs you something. But when you sow an offering out of obedience to the Scripture, and because of the prompting of the Holy Spirit, *God will return what you gave to Him in money or what money cannot buy*. Kristi found this to be true as she was asking for her daily bread.

4. Daily Bread

Jesus taught us to pray *each day* for daily bread, just like Moses and the children of Israel received their daily portion of manna. He said to ask daily, to be specific with God—"What do you want Me to do for you?" (Mark 10:51)—and to be tenacious—keep on seeking, asking, and knocking until the door is opened to you. That was exactly what Kristi had been doing for some time since she had learned how to effectively pray through the Lord's Prayer. But today, as she asked for her "daily bread," God gave her a word—*living* "bread"— to help her obtain her *financial* "bread." This is the letter she shared with me:

In February, 1990, the Lord spoke to me in prayer one day as I asked Him why my life hadn't changed much. I was still broke, owed everyone, my oldest son was in another state in a home for boys, my body was sick, I had very little hope. The answer to me was, "You are robbing me, you are cursed with a curse." I said, "I am? I didn't know. I didn't mean to rob you." Then I felt impressed to read Mal. 3. Afterwards, I replied, "I've always given 10% tithes, and an offering when I could." He said, "You have not given me a *full measure* in your *offering*. I can't give a full measure of blessing to you, if you don't give a full measure in your offering." Then the Holy Spirit led me through the Scriptures showing me how to understand the Lord's view of unjust weights and measures, and showed me the specific amount that He desired for me to be obedient in giving.

I thought, since I hardly have any money now, when I get some extra I will do this. Big mistake! Six weeks later I was completely broke, about to be evicted from my apartment, my car wouldn't run, my hope was lost, and my life was going from bad to worse. I cried out to God, "What's wrong?" and He reminded me of our previous conversation. So at this point I began giving full tithes out of every little bit I received, gladly, and the offering He had instructed me as a point of obedience.

In four weeks, my pastor spoke this word to me: "God is adding to you." I thought, "O.K., I receive." But the next few weeks were the longest in my life. Then suddenly things started to happen: someone gave me two beds; we had been sleeping on the floor. I began saying, "God is adding to me!" Next my four-year-old and I were invited on a week vacation to Orlando. "God is adding to me!" I said. The day we left, my lawyer called and made this surprise announcement: "After 1½ years, your case has settled. Come pick up your money. You don't even have to wait ten days; you get it today." The amount was $12,000! What a vacation we had!

When we returned home, I received word that I could move into a spacious 2-bedroom apartment for just a little more than I currently paid for my small one. God was continuing to add to me!

On Wednesday night of the same week, I prayed, "Lord, I can't find a car to drive. If you want me to have a newer car please set me in the middle of it. I want to honor you and pay cash." As I shopped for cars the following day, I began to hear, "The blessing of the Lord makes rich and adds no sorrow to it." All of these cars had sorrow; they were too expensive and not what I needed. Finally, I found the car which was right, but the price advertised in the paper was $5,000. I was determined to spend only $4,000. After three hours of waiting, the Lord moved on the heart of the owner of the dealership, and he said, "O.K., you can have it for $4,000." Praise God! *It's loaded—with no sorrow!* The Lord honored me back.

That night, after I was in bed, the phone rang at 1:00 A.M. It was my son in California. He said, "Mom, I'm coming home tomorrow." He was taken from me in a court case when he was two; he's sixteen now. God is so good. He is adding to me!

P.S. Part of my settlement is two years free college, and placement in a new career. I start in June.

I also received two years free medical for my back.

This precious lady had been obedient in her giving for years but learned an invaluable faith lesson concerning her offering. When you give in response to the promptings of the Holy Spirit, according to the Word of God, it will not hurt you but will "make a way" for you through your wilderness. You can rest assured that God will return your sacrifice to Him, in money or what money cannot buy.

As Larry has so often said, "You cannot lose if you do not quit."

Desperate to Be Secure

Growing up an abused child of an alcoholic, Karen had lived an uncertain and scary life. Security was elusive, something she always longed for, yet never possessed. When Robert came on the scene— tall, blond, handsome, and *strong*—she believed her knight in shining armor had appeared. But even though he tried to be her emotional support, Robert could not fulfill the deep need in her heart. Finances were a constant battle, and soon he was smoking four to five joints a day just to ease the pressure.

Karen also had a drug and alcohol problem, which was bad enough in itself, but since she was a nurse employed in ICU, it almost proved fatal. One night while on duty and high on marijuana, she accidentally gave a patient the wrong medication. Although he survived, Karen was devastated. She had always prided herself on being a compassionate, responsible nurse, but now she was out of control. She could not even trust herself for this source of security. Her depression was so complete that as she described it: "I felt like I was being pulled down into a black hole."

Just a few weeks prior, Karen and Robert had received the most unusual letter in the mail. An elderly gentleman who had picked their name out of the phone book had written them a letter telling them about the goodness of God. Karen had read and reread its wonderful words before she ever showed it to Robert. Her heart was strangely stirred.

Then the terrible incident at the hospital occurred. Unable to function, and all that she had ever trusted in destroyed, Karen called her mother-in-law, looking for one last shred of hope. These were the words that penetrated her darkness: "What you're looking for is found only in Jesus."

After several days of the intense dealings of God, Karen released her sin and insecurities to Jesus. She began to devour the Word of God; it became living, daily bread to her famished soul. She clung to the promises of God like a dying woman. She had to—things had gone from bad to worse, and now she and Robert were separated. But as she prayed for him declaring God's promises, Robert's heart began to be melted, and soon, he, too, turned his life over to Jesus. But this is no fairy tale; they did not live happily ever after. Immediately thereafter Robert lost his job and thus began a terrible four-year battle with finances. Through it all, Karen and Robert determined that if they had no money for anything else, they would not get into worse trouble by robbing God. So regardless of what came in that month, they tithed. During this time, they lost their car, their home, and $30,000 in equity to the IRS. Bill collectors called daily. Their daughter was on drugs and tried to commit suicide; their son was in drug rehabilitation.

In 1986, Murphy's Law had gone just about its full limit with them. It was Christmas, and they had *no* money with which to buy presents. They had endeavored to have a garage sale just to have enough to buy groceries. But regardless of their financial catastrophes, they were determined to give something to the Lord for Christmas. The only belongings they continued to possess of any value were two treasured sentimental pieces: a pair of diamond earrings that Robert had given to Karen and an 18 karat gold chain that she had given to him. These they quietly dropped into an offering envelope and gave them to the Lord on Christmas Sunday morning.

God saw their actions, but much more, He saw their hearts. Their tithes and sacrificial giving had come up before Him as a memorial, just as the scriptural account of Cornelius (see Acts 10). The heavenlies began to move on their behalf. Their children's lives began to settle down: their daughter quit drugs and was reunited with her husband and two children; their son gave his life to Jesus. Within a month, they had birthed a God idea: their own business—a nursing and respiratory therapy agency. It was blessed: in 1987 they were able to give more in tithes and offerings than they had *made* the year before. At the close of 1990, they were able to pay out $1.4 million in salaries to their employees.

"I determined not to limit God with unbelief," declared Karen. "I resolved instead to believe His Word. Every day I asked Him to give me my daily bread. Every time He gave me some income, I gave Him His part. Even in the hardest times, when it looked like there was no help or hope, Robert and I clung to God's promises and declared them over our lives. Now look how God has blessed us! We just pray now for wisdom to know how to be a blessing with what He's entrusted to us."

Karen knows that riches are as uncertain as life is apart from the promises of God. She would urge you, "When riches increase, don't set your heart on them, for they might take wings and fly away. Put your trust and security in the Word of God, which lives and abides forever."

George Muller, the great man of prayer, left a great legacy in the earth to the faithfulness of God concerning provision for those who lived in obedience to His commands and daily trusted in His promises. He wrote in his diary,

> I longed to set something before the children of God, whereby they might see, that *He does not forsake, even in our day, those who rely upon Him. . . . To show them by proofs* that He is the same in our day.
> It needed to be something which could be seen, even by the natural eye. Now, if I, a poor man, simply by prayer and faith,

obtained, *without asking any individual,* the means for establishing and carrying on an Orphan House, there would be something which, with the Lord's blessing, might be instrumental in strengthening the faith of the children of God, besides being a testimony to the consciences of the unconverted, of the reality of the things of God. This, then, was the primary reason for establishing the Orphan House.

The realities of life for a child born in Muller's day in England were grim. Children as young as five years of age worked from 6:00 A.M. to 8:00 P.M. six days a week in the tobacco factories, potteries, or coal tunnels, dragging heavy loads of coal. Those who escaped lived in the streets by their wits, which usually meant by stealing.

Each day Muller prayed and believed God's promises; each day God provided. On one occasion he wrote: "Never were we so reduced in funds as today. There was not a single halfpenny in hand between the matrons of the three houses. Nevertheless there was a good dinner." On another occasion he wrote, "There was given by a stranger, a sovereign for the orphans, which I received today. Thus the Lord has again begun the week with mercy, and His love surely will help us through it, though again many pounds will be needed." Muller later testified, "The orphans never lacked anything. Had I thousands of pounds in hand, they would have fared no better than they have; for they have always had good, nourishing food, the necessary articles of clothings, etc."

A. J. Rendle Short observed,

> The scientific agnostics of the Victorian era, T. H. Huxley,
> J. Tyndall and the rest, poured scorn on the idea that praying makes
> any difference to the course of events, but their theories did not get
> any great hold in Bristol, under the shadow of the Ashley Down
> Orphanage. As a donor wrote, it might be interesting if Professor
> Huxley and his sympathisers who thought prayer a mere waste of
> breath would try how long they could keep an orphanage going
> with over 2,000 orphans without asking anyone for help.

Muller once said, "Oh! how kind is the Lord. Always, before there has been actual want, He has sent help."

John Howe remarked in "Treatise of Delight in God": "Consider that your condition on earth is such as exposes you to many sufferings and hardships, which by your not delighting in him, you can never be sure to avoid (for they are things common to men), but which by your delighting in him, you may be easily able to endure."

King David wrote in Psalm 37:25, "I have been young, and now am old; yet I have not seen the righteous forsaken, nor his descendants begging bread." "He doth not say," commented Joseph Caryl in C. H. Spurgeon's *The Treasury of David,* "'in my experience I never saw the righteous *afflicted,* but, I never saw him *left* or *forsaken in his affliction.*'"

Although you may never have the testimony of Mary Crowley, Kristi, or Karen, through prayer and obedience you should be able to say with George Muller, "Oh, how kind is the Lord. Always, before there has been actual want, He has sent help."

Proverbs 30:8–9 says,

> Give me neither poverty nor riches—
> Feed me with the food allotted to me;
> Lest I be full and deny You,
> And say, "Who is the LORD?"
> Or lest I be poor and steal,
> And profane the name of my God.

God alone knows the level of blessing you are able to receive, and His ear is ever open to your cry, His hand waiting to move in response to your faith and obedience.

Don't forsake your own mercy. Pray as Jesus taught you: "Give me *this day* my daily bread." Be specific; be tenacious; believe His promises; sow your seed. Then expect your need to be supplied from His hand.

The Lord said, "I know the thoughts that I think toward you, . . . thoughts of peace and not of evil, to give you a future and a hope" (Jer. 29:1). Now you have a foundation for *real* security!

10 Desperate to Be Forgiven

"And forgive us our debts . . ."

While we were still sinners, Christ died for us.

—Romans 5:8

Where sin abounded, grace abounded much more.

—Romans 5:20

When she was three years old, Roseanne was branded inside her vagina and dedicated by her parents and grandparents to Satan. Her upbringing was not the norm. She witnessed and suffered years of unspeakable abuse to break her will and bring her to a place of servitude under the ruler of darkness. As is often the case, the abused became the abuser.

By the time she was nine, Roseanne was willingly taking part in ritualistic blood sacrifices in order to escape some of the abuse herself. During her teens, she became pregnant five times, once by her father; that baby was aborted and its body used in a satanic rite. Three other babies were carried full term, only to become human sacrifices.

Years of utter depravity, experiencing and administering torture, knowing nothing but death, darkness, fear, and horror resulted in her total dehumanization. Not knowing any other way out of her living hell, never having experienced love in any form, and not daring to even imagine that there could be a way of forgiveness and redemption for her, Roseanne chose the only way of escape that she knew—she blocked out everything through mental illness.

Declared "hopeless" by six psychiatrists, Roseanne was thrust out upon society where she became a street person. Although she was indoctrinated to believe that there was no God, His merciful hand reached down to her.

Her only child, a son who had escaped the fate of his brothers and sisters, was now five years old. On Sundays while Roseanne slept off the effects of drugs and alcohol, the bus from a local church began to pick up the lonely little boy. He came home telling his mother wonderful stories of Jesus and His love, and of His power to change lives. In vicious anger, Roseanne responded by beating him. Nonetheless, when the bus rolled around the next Sunday, the little boy again climbed aboard.

Soon he was outside in the courtyard preaching Bible stories to the neighborhood children. Simultaneously, God sent a lovely Christian woman into Roseanne's life. This woman was unlike any Roseanne had ever known before. She exhibited real love. She fasted and prayed for her and invited her to church on numerous occasions. Roseanne's only reply was, "I'm gonna kill you," to which the woman answered, "I can't do anything but love you."

Finally, partially out of intrigue—wondering what made this woman so different—and partially just to silence her persistent invitations, Roseanne agreed to attend a church service with her. She was completely unprepared for what she encountered.

Totally terrified by the unfamiliar love she saw and felt, Roseanne nevertheless began to be drawn to its Source. Could it be that there was a way out of the impenetrable darkness that had been her life? Up until that moment, Roseanne had never actually considered that there might be a way of finding forgiveness for all the atrocities in which she had participated. She thought that she was beyond hope, with no right to believe for redemption. And then, she heard the truly good news of Jesus, the One chosen by God, who willingly took her sin—all of her horrible, rotten, stinking, filthy sin—and gave her a brand-new life. Oh, the depths of the love and mercy of God! For the first time since she was three years old, Roseanne began to cry. Through her tears of repentance before God, the sin and degradation, shame and guilt began to be broken off her hardened spirit. She experienced God's love not only around her but *in* her. She was born anew.

I would like to tell you that Roseanne's deliverance was complete and instantaneous in that moment, but her journey out of hell was not an overnight experience. Her road to healing was a rocky one, with many faithful members of her church gathering around her to pray with her and to support her through the tough times. Still, Roseanne discovered that He who had begun a good work in her *was and is* faithful!

He had been faithful to His Word in forgiving her: "If we confess our sins, He is faithful and just to forgive us our sins and to cleanse us from all unrighteousness" (1 John 1:9).

Roseanne also saw God's faithfulness in a day by day, moment by moment experience. Philippians 1:6 became a reality in her life: "He who has begun a good work in you will complete it until the day of Jesus Christ."

Clean and sober now for several years, Roseanne stands as a "sign and wonder" for all who need to experience the depths of the love and forgiveness of God. She personifies the words of Jesus when He said, "She who has been forgiven much loves much." A radiant Christian, a faithful church member, and an experienced intercessor in the prayer army, Roseanne now shares her testimony and ministers to groups across the nation about the power of God's love and forgiveness. When I interviewed her for this book, she said, "Tell the women, 'Your circumstances may be different from mine, but your hurt is no less deep to you than mine was to me. If God can forgive me, He can forgive you, too.'"

The story of the good news of Jesus Christ begins with the words, "While we were *still sinners,* Christ died for us." God sent His Son, Jesus, to die for us not because we were *good* but because we were *sinners*. It is the woman in the pit who needs a rope thrown to her. It is the woman drowning at sea who needs a lifeline. It is the sinner who needs a Savior.

The apostle Paul wrote, "Jesus Christ came . . . to save sinners," and then added a personal note, "of whom I am chief" (1 Tim. 1:15). He knew whereof he spoke: he had been responsible for the deaths of many men, women, and children—saints of God—in the years before his conversion. But after his life-changing encounter with Jesus, he was able to write with insight birthed out of personal experience, "While we were still sinners, Christ died for us." He further wrote,

> When we were utterly helpless with no way of escape, Christ
> came at just the right time and died for us sinners who had no use
> for him. Even if we were good, we really wouldn't expect anyone to
> die for us, though, of course, that might be barely possible. But God
> showed his great love for us by sending Christ to die for us while
> we were still sinners" (Rom. 5:6–8 TLB).

Face Up to Sin

For a number of years now, the word *sin* has been considered archaic and passé, and those who used it, totally out of touch with reality. Our technologically advanced, computerized, impersonal, hedonistic society that adheres to the doctrine "I'm O.K., you're O.K." has ignored the big *S* word, pretending it does not exist. But exist it does, in an increasingly arrogant and flagrant manner. Ignoring sin does not make it disappear. It does not change the ruined circumstances. It does not heal the broken heart. Ignoring sin does not bring triumphant life into the place of death.

The Bible warns repeatedly about false prophets, those who would declare to us, "Peace, peace, when there is no peace." Oh, how we need to be aware of those false words today! A woman knows when she is feeling guilt or shame. She knows when she is frustrated that her inner life doesn't match up with her outward behavior. She knows when she has caused pain to another person or to herself. She has no peace. Yet, dozens of voices in her world every day will proclaim falsely to her:

"Oh, it's O.K. It's not really all that bad what you did and said."

"It'll be all right. Just forget it."

"Well, what do you expect? God made you that way, and it's just part of your human weakness."

"Things will get better. Just give it some time."

"Everybody's doing it. It can't be bad."

"You've got to try some things in order to know what's going on and be sophisticated."

"Peace, peace" . . . but there is no peace.

A woman is deceived, too, when she thinks, *Well, I'm not an axe murderer. I've never robbed a bank. I've never done anything of such evil magnitude in my life. I'm not a sinner. I'm a* good *person.* That line of reasoning doesn't excuse anyone from the truth that "all have sinned and fall short of the glory of God" (Rom. 3:23).

From the vilest, most perverted individual to the precious child with a cherubic winsome disposition—"*all* have sinned." The Bible teaches that in sin our mothers conceived us. We were brought forth in iniquity. We came forth out of the womb speaking lies. The truth is not in us (see Ps. 51).

The apostle Paul described our inbred sinful condition this way:

> I don't understand myself at all, for I really want to do what is right, but I can't. I do what I don't want to—what I hate. I know perfectly well that what I am doing is wrong, and my bad conscience proves that I agree with these laws I am breaking. But I can't help myself, because I'm no longer doing it. It is sin inside me that is stronger than I am that makes me do these evil things.

I know I am rotten through and through so far as my old sinful nature is concerned. No matter which way I turn I can't make myself do right. I want to but I can't. When I want to do good, I don't; and when I try not to do wrong, I do it anyway. Now if I am doing what I don't want to, it is plain where the trouble is: sin . . . has me in its evil grasp (Rom. 7:15-20 TLB).

Dr. Charles Stanley of First Baptist Church in Atlanta wrote this about our sinful nature:

Our sin causes us to "fall short." Our sin disqualifies us in light of God's standard. Sins put us in a relationship with God wherein we owe Him something. We must pay for what we have done much like criminals must repay society for the crimes they have committed. Thus, the solution must in some way remove the consequences of our sin and restore us to a state in which our sin is no longer counted against us. Somehow what was done through sin must be undone. So, how can that happen? How can the sinful be made the sinless?

Could such a marvelous idea be possible? After all, "the wages of sin [the end result, the payment owed to God] is death" (Rom. 6:23). And "sin, when it is fullgrown, brings forth death" (James 1:15).

If I am born with a sin nature, am unable to keep from sinning even against my own human will, and am facing a death sentence from God for my sin, where is my hope? I cry just as the apostle Paul cried at that realization: "Oh, what a terrible predicament I'm in! Who will free me from my slavery to this deadly lower nature? Thank God! *It has been done by Jesus Christ our Lord.* He has set me free!" (Rom. 7:24-25 TLB).

The apostle Paul further describes the freedom won for us by Jesus Christ, likening our sinful nature to Adam, the father of human sin:

And since by his blood he did all this for us as sinners, how much more will he do for us now that he has declared us not guilty? Now he will save us from all of God's wrath to come. . . .

When Adam sinned, sin entered the entire human race. . . . For this one man, Adam, brought death to many through his *sin*. But this one man, Jesus Christ, brought forgiveness to many through God's mercy. Adam's *one* sin brought the penalty of death to many, while Christ freely takes away *many* sins and gives glorious life instead. The sin of this one man, Adam, caused *death to be king over all,* but all who will take God's gift of forgiveness and acquittal are *kings of life* because of this one man, Jesus Christ. Yes, Adam's *sin* brought *punishment* to all, but Christ's *righteousness* makes men *right with God,* so that they can live. Adam caused many to be sinners because he *disobeyed* God, and Christ caused many to be made acceptable to God because he *obeyed* (Rom. 5:9, 12, 15–19 TLB).

From being guilty to being not guilty.

From a death penalty to a full pardon.

From a position where death is king over us to a position where we are kings over life.

From punishment to right standing with God.

That is what Jesus Christ has done for us!

We do not need to hear false words of "peace, peace" as some kind of frosting on the cake of our sin. We need to hear "repentance, forgiveness" as a means of totally renewing all that we are, pardoning all that we have done, restoring all that we have lost, and putting us into position to receive more of life than we have ever imagined!

"Where," you may ask, "is the entering in place to this type of forgiveness? How can I experience this cleaning from my guilt and shame? How can I receive this gift of God?"

First, you must accept the fact that you are a sinner in need of forgiveness. Often, it is not the person who has committed the heinous or occultic crime who has trouble realizing the need of forgiveness but the individual who has led a relatively "clean" life. A family friend once had occasion to question a leading religious leader in our community—a man much admired for his social activism—with these words: "Are you saved?"

The man responded, "Saved from what? I don't need to be saved."

This man had never faced the reality of his own sins!

Turn and confront your sins. Don't try to outrun them, which you'll never be able to do. You can run and run from the truth of your sinful nature but never escape the nagging, gnawing darkness within.

Face up to the fact, "I have sinned and come short of the glory of God."

Elisabeth Elliot wrote in *Let Me Be a Woman,* "You do need forgiveness . . . and it is a wonderfully healing thing to confess your sin . . . and to ask for . . . forgiveness."

Receive God's Provision

Second, you must be willing to receive *God's* provision for forgiveness. We often have an unnatural bent toward penance. Innately, we know that when we sin, something must be done to make things right. We miss the mark, however, when we attempt within our flesh to do something of merit that, *we hope,* will put us in right standing with God. We try to make up for our sins by doing something noble or obviously good in our own eyes. The more we try to dig ourselves out of our own mud pit of sin, the muddier we get! The Bible says that God's only recognized provision for our sin is the blood of Jesus. Not our works. Not what we consider to be our righteous deeds. As the old hymn goes, "What can wash away my sin?/Nothing but the blood of Jesus."

You really have only one choice. You can accept Jesus' death on the cross as the sacrifice for your sin, or you can reject it. God has no Plan B for your salvation. His Plan A—the blood of Jesus—is sufficient, covers all your sin, and is the only way.

Hebrews 9:22 says, "Without the shedding of blood there is no forgiveness" (NIV). Try as we might to come up with an acceptable substitute, we are faced again and again with the fact that God has established: "My Son's shed blood is the only means of forgiveness that I will accept."

Dr. Stanley wrote in his book *Forgiveness:*

> We did not have the potential to regain for ourselves what was necessary to make us acceptable to God. It was checkmate; the game was over; there were no more moves for us to make. And it was nobody's fault but our own. Yet in our darkest hour, God gave us an extra Player and, in doing so, a second chance.

We are not in a position to make up the rules for our own forgiveness. God has already established them.

Jesus took upon Himself your sins—all of them—past, present, and future. He experienced your punishment—total separation from God, the terror of the death of the damned, and consignment to hell. But hell had no *legal* claim on Him personally. He had never sinned. The punishment He received was for *your sins and mine,* not His! He was the sinlessly perfect, sacrificial Lamb. As a result, Jesus Christ could demand the keys of death and hell from the devil and get them! He could ascend back to the right hand of the throne of God with all the privileges and power of lordship. He, alone, can now be your sympathetic High Priest and Lawyer in heaven.

No Sin Too Great

Furthermore, no sin is too great to be covered by His sacrifice on the cross. No case is "too tough" for Him to defend as our Advocate in heaven.

In 2 Chronicles 33 we read about a man who was perhaps the most notorious sinner of all time: Manasseh. The Scriptures say that Manasseh "did evil in the sight of the LORD, according to the abominations of the nations whom the LORD had cast out before the children of Israel" (2 Chron. 33:2). He rebuilt the altars to the false gods and made wooden images of the Baals. He worshiped the stars of heaven and let astrology dictate his life. He caused his sons to be sacrificed and to "pass through the fire." He practiced soothsaying, witchcraft, and sorcery, and he consulted mediums and spiritists. He went so far as to set up an idol in the temple. But that still wasn't all.

Manasseh "seduced Judah and the inhabitants of Jerusalem to do more evil than the nations whom the LORD had destroyed before the children of Israel" (2 Chron. 33:9).

The Lord spoke to Manasseh and his people, but they wouldn't listen. Finally, Manasseh was captured by the king of Assyria and taken in bronze fetters to Babylon.

What was the fate of this evil man?

The Bible says that "when he was in affliction, he implored the LORD his God, and humbled himself greatly before the God of his fathers, and prayed to Him; and He received his entreaty, heard his supplication, and brought him back to Jerusalem into his kingdom" (2 Chron. 33:12–13). God gave Manasseh a second chance. And Manasseh took away the foreign gods, repaired the altar of the Lord, and led Judah in serving the Lord God of Israel!

Whatever sin *you* may have committed, it's not too great for God to reverse it and to forgive you when you call out to Him!

Conversely, no sin is too small for God's forgiveness. There's no such thing as a "white lie" or a "little sin." Sin is sin. All of it stains us and separates us from God.

No matter the nature or magnitude of your sin, run to the Cross with it. Accept God's provision for your forgiveness.

Not a Feeling, a Fact

Forgiveness is cleansing. Oh, what joy to be clean! We know that in a physical way, don't we? After days of camping out, we can hardly wait to get home to a hot shower. A spiritual cleansing brings with it cause for deep, abiding joy!

"But," you may say, "I don't *feel* forgiven."

Forgiveness may bring feeling, but feeling isn't a necessary part of forgiveness.

As Dr. Stanley has said, "Being forgiven has nothing to do with feeling forgiven." Being forgiven has to do with what God died for you on the Cross. When you confess your sinful nature to God and declare, "Oh, God, I confess to You that I am a sinner. I need the blood of Jesus to wash away my sins. I accept His sacrifice for me. Have mercy on me and forgive me!"—then God is true to His own Word and forgives you.

Renewing Salvation Daily

Then every day thereafter that you pray, "Forgive us our debts," you are in a position of renewing your salvation. You're updating your forgiveness, revalidating your forgiveness. You stand daily and admit that your nature is to sin, that you don't want to sin, that you look to the shed blood of Jesus to cover your sins and restore you to right standing with God, and that you need to be forgiven. And daily, God is faithful to do that work in you. He stands ever ready to hear your confession so that the blood of Jesus might avail and prevail. He promises, "Whosoever comes to Me, I will in no wise cast her out."

Whether it is your first time to come to His feet and seek forgiveness or the ten thousandth time you have stood in daily prayer and humbly asked, "Forgive me my debts," He will forgive.

Are you desperate to be forgiven?

Know today that He can forgive you. He longs to forgive you. He has made provision to forgive you. And He is ready to forgive you right now. You only need to ask Him!

11 Desperate to Forgive

". . . As we forgive our debtors."

I am convinced that we do not learn to forgive in the hour of crisis,
we actually train for it. It is something you train for in the easy
times and in the small things so that you can perform graciously in
the difficult times.

—Gail MacDonald

Be kind to one another, tenderhearted, forgiving one another, even as
God in Christ forgave you.

—Ephesians 4:32

Tribulation. We all have it. If it's not one thing, it's another. Just as
we've solved one problem, another one seems to be coming over the
horizon. It's always something.

God isn't surprised. He never promised us that it would be any
other way. In fact, Jesus said, "In the world you *will* have tribulation." He also said, "Offenses *will* come."

This is not to say that God sends these tribulations and offenses.
They are a part of our fallen humanity and, in some cases, a direct
assault of the enemy. It is to say that God has made a way for us to live
through tribulation and come out on top. He has made a way for us to
face offenses and use them as stepping-stones to a greater plateau of
Christian living rather than trip over offenses as stumbling stones.

Jesus could speak with authority on the issue of tribulation because
He faced it on a daily basis. He had multiple opportunities to become
offended. His own cousin, the mighty prophet of God, John the
Baptist—who had seen the Holy Spirit descend on Jesus and who had
declared Him to be the Holy Lamb of God—later doubted who Jesus
was. The Pharisees said that Jesus was demon possessed and that He

performed miracles through witchcraft; they sought every possible opportunity to ensnare Him in His words. His own mother and brothers thought He was crazy. The multitudes who followed Him were more interested in the bread that He provided freely rather than the Bread of Life He embodied.

And then there were the Twelve. The ones who lived with Him and saw His life in all circumstances. The ones who were taught the hidden meanings of the parables. The ones who were eyewitnesses to His miracles. What a joy and comfort they turned out to be!

When Jesus rebuked the Pharisees, calling them hypocrites, the disciples feared for their own reputations. When Jesus came to them walking on the water, they thought He was a ghost. When Moses and Elijah appeared with Him as He was transfigured before their eyes, they wanted to build a tabernacle and worship all three as coequals, actually bringing Jesus, the Son of God, down to the level of being a great *man*. When He broke the news to them that He was about to die, rather than add to His comfort, they added to His grief by arguing among themselves who was going to be the greatest when He finally established His kingdom.

Such are the joys of the ministry, of working with people, and of living as Christians in this world. Offenses will come. And furthermore, once today's batch has passed, more are on the way! Yes, it's an "always something" world in which we live!

When Jesus most needed the love and prayer support of His closest friends, they went to sleep. When He was arrested, all of them ran, cowering in fear lest they, too, be implicated. When He was arraigned before Pilate, they were nowhere to be seen. He was left to experience torture and death by crucifixion . . . except for John who accompanied Mary, Jesus' mother, to the foot of the cross.

If anyone ever had reason to harbor, even nurture, a root of bitterness, it was Jesus. And yet, the writer of Hebrews encourages with these words:

> Let us lay aside every weight, and the sin which so easily
> ensnares us, . . . looking unto Jesus, the author and finisher of our
> faith. . . . For *consider Him who endured such hostility from sinners
> against Himself, lest you become weary and discouraged in your
> souls. You have not yet resisted to bloodshed, striving against sin*
> (Heb. 12:1–4, emphasis added).

To find out how not to give in to bitterness, we look to Jesus! He didn't give in to bitterness, even though offenses and tribulation led all the way to a cruel death. Because He didn't give in and because He lives in us, we don't need to give in to bitterness, either! We can live through tribulation and above offense!

What was Jesus' secret for dealing with daily offenses? He said, "Forgive us our sins—*as we forgive those who sin against us*."

Once we have experienced the blessed forgiveness of God, none of us wants to let a day go past without a renewed assurance that we stand forgiven. But in order for this to be so, we must be willing to forgive those who sin against us. Just as we surely will sin every day and need God's forgiveness for our sins every day, so others will sin against us and need our forgiveness on a daily basis. Our slate cannot be cleared before God if we willfully refuse to forgive and choose instead to cling to and nurse our anger, hurt, bitterness, and resentment.

How much are we called upon to forgive others? Jesus addressed this question specifically.

The disciples were in disagreement among themselves, arguing about which one of them was the greatest and deserving of the most power. Peter, always the most outspoken, was the one who had first discerned that Jesus was "the Christ, the Son of the living God" (John 6:69). Surely he would be chief among them! James and John were in the inner circle, and everyone knew that John was Jesus' favorite. Would they be given the authority and place of honor their mother had come to request? And then there was Judas. Since he controlled the money, shouldn't he control the entire organization? Andrew was the first to be called by Jesus. Would he have the first seat? And on it went, each one thinking of himself more highly than he ought—a common malady today, too!

Peter, feeling particularly self-righteous, approached Jesus with this question: "Lord, how many times should I forgive my brother? *Seven* times?" I'm sure Peter thought he was being considerably magnanimous since the rabbis required only that a man forgive three times. Jesus shot Peter's pompous, parsimonious bubble full of holes. "Not just seven times, Peter," Jesus calmly replied, "but *seventy times seven*."

Then Jesus continued with this parable within the hearing of all His disciples:

> The Kingdom of Heaven can be compared to a king who decided to bring his accounts up to date. In the process, one of his debtors

was brought in who owed him $10,000,000! He couldn't pay, so the king ordered him sold for the debt, also his wife and children and everything he had.

But the man fell down before the king, his face in the dust, and said, "Oh, sir, be patient with me and I will pay it all."

Then the king was filled with pity for him and released him and forgave his debt.

But when the man left the king, he went to a man who owed him $2,000 and grabbed him by the throat and demanded instant payment.

The man fell down before him and begged him to give him a little time. "Be patient and I will pay it," he pled.

But his creditor wouldn't wait. He had the man arrested and jailed until the debt would be paid in full.

Then the man's friends went to the king and told him what had happened. And the king called before him the man he had forgiven and said, "You evil-hearted wretch! Here I forgave you all that tremendous debt, just because you asked me to—shouldn't you have mercy on others, just as I had mercy on you?"

Then the angry king sent the man to the torture chamber until he had paid every last penny due. So shall my heavenly Father do to you if you refuse to truly forgive your brothers (Matt. 18:23–35 TLB).

The disciples no doubt dropped their heads in shame at Jesus' words, remembering another time when the Master had taught them to pray, adding as if to underscore and emphasize one part of the prayer, "Remember, if you do not forgive, you cannot be forgiven" (see Matt. 6:14–15).

As they pondered His parable, the disciples were no doubt struck with the thought, *Could any grudge hold water as a good excuse to withhold forgiveness?* The answer to them and to us is no.

In sum, we are faced with the fact that we MUST forgive those who offend us. Why? Because Jesus said so, in order for us to be forgiven. He didn't state any offense that was beyond that rule of forgiveness; He didn't provide any loopholes; He didn't offer any disclaimers or any other method. Jesus said, "This is the way to be truly forgiven: forgive."

Jesus did not teach His disciples in words alone. He was their example. A few weeks later, His words from the cross rang out clear and strong: "Father, forgive them, for they do not know what they do" (Luke 23:34). Even dying as an innocent man—the most inno-

cent of all, utterly without sin and guile—Jesus could and did forgive.
Mary Crowley wrote in *A Pocketful of Miracles,*

> This is what is commonly called the first word from Jesus on the
> cross. The first word is a word of forgiveness. Isn't it precious to
> know that the first thought in the heart of Jesus was a thought of
> forgiveness? The entire act of salvation, the entire day of the
> crucifixion was to be centered on forgiveness. . . . "Father forgive
> these people, for they do not know what they are doing." . . . Even
> in agony, in heartbreak and sorrow, Jesus wanted to grant
> forgiveness!

Jesus had been in training in the art of forgiveness all His life, and
especially so in the last three years. By choosing to forgive the daily
offenses against Him, He was prepared for the most difficult test of
His ability to forgive. As Gail MacDonald puts it, He "performed
graciously."

Through the travail of His soul in prayer while in the Garden of
Gethsemane, Jesus also had received grace to set His will toward the
completion of what the Father had placed before Him, and thus, He
was later enabled to plead, "Father, forgive them." In so doing, Jesus
exemplified to His disciples and to us that forgiveness is not a matter
of the emotions but a choice of the will. Once the will is set, the
emotions will sooner or later fall into line. We must choose to forgive.

Have others offended you today? Are you experiencing tribulation
because of what others have done or said against you? Have you *chosen* to forgive?

A Choice of the Will

Victor Frankl, who endured the most horrible evil one can ever
experience in his personal tribulation as a Jew in Nazi concentration
camps, wrote, "Everything can be taken away from a man but one
thing: the last of human freedoms—to choose one's attitude in any
given set of circumstances." Even as a horribly mistreated prisoner,
Frankl chose to forgive and to have an attitude of freedom. In so
doing, he was more free than his captors.

When Jesus set His will to forgive and later cried, "Father, forgive
them," He became our consummate example of forgiveness for all
time. Not only did He become the *means* of our forgiveness by God,

He became our example of how to forgive others. Oswald Chambers said, "We talk glibly about forgiving when we have never been injured; when we are injured we know that it is not possible, apart from God's grace, for one human being to forgive another." But Jesus had been repeatedly injured, and repeatedly, He chose to forgive. He was injured without cause. Yes, we *can* look unto Him and "consider Him who endured such hostility from sinners against Himself" (Heb. 12:3) and not be wearied or faint in our minds at the thought of forgiving those who bring offense against us.

When Are You Harboring an Offense?

How can you tell when you are harboring unforgiveness? You will be in torment. When you're taking a shower, your thoughts will turn toward the person and the offense you have felt. You find it difficult to pray. You feel upset continually, talking to yourself in the mirror about the offense, and lie awake or awaken in the middle of the night with the incident or the relationship on your mind. The memory of the offense grows stronger the more you rehearse it in your mind; the aggravation remains intense hour after hour, day after day; you feel anger (or intense dismay or hurt) at the mention of the person's name; you begin to wish that something bad would happen to that person. As the saying goes, "The more you stir it, the more it stinks."

Those are all signals not for Valium or Rolaids but for forgiveness! You are suffering from an offense, and you are in danger of developing a root of bitterness that will ultimately destroy your soul.

In 1987, a broken, devastated, desperate woman and her two sons found their way to our church. Jill had just been released from a psychiatric floor of a hospital. She had lost everything she ever held dear: her self-esteem, husband, daughter, family, home, business, friends, and health. Not knowing where else to turn—indeed, not having anywhere else to turn—she turned to the Lord, and gradually as she began to learn how to pray and to forgive, she found solace for her grief. Hope sprang alive once more in her heart. Here is the story she recently told me:

"Seven years ago, I thought my life was finally on an uphill climb. I had been through one bad marriage, during which time I had three children, but my new relationship had lasted for ten years and I thought we were doing fine. Life's storms seemed to have passed, and I was proud of the stability of mind I felt and the life-style I had been able to create.

"My daughter Amy, age fourteen, came to live with me, and I was delighted when my husband, Jimmy, reached out to her and tried to make up for the years Amy had not known a father. I overlooked the fact that he favored her over the boys; I failed to notice the little escapades of their wrestling on the floor. As the months went by, the atmosphere of our home changed to one of increasing strife. I knew something was wrong, but I couldn't put the pieces together. Then Amy became pregnant. The father of her child was my husband.

"The rage that I felt in the wake of a year of deceit was probably the culmination of all the pain I had ever suffered. Amy had already left the house when the news of her pregnancy was presented to me. In blind rage, I readily admit that I lost all control. I destroyed everything in my daughter's room that had been dear to her. I wanted nothing to remind me of her. I actually committed murder in my heart toward my only daughter. I put all of the blame on her, since Jimmy had been the most moral, trustworthy person I had ever known.

"My physical rampage ended within a few hours but a mental and emotional anger continued to simmer. I was tormented every hour of the day both in sleeping and in waking. Mental pictures replayed over and over in my mind. And I justified every feeling that I had. After all, I had been betrayed by two of the people I trusted most in all my world.

"One day while wallowing in self-pity, justification, and torment, I heard James Robison say, 'If we harbor bitterness and will not forgive, we are given over to the tormentors.' He went on to say that we have to take charge of our own will and obey God in forgiving, even if we don't feel like it. I chose to face my situation head-on. I didn't like the idea of living with torment the rest of my life.

"I brought my daughter home to live with me. Actually, at the time, I had hoped I could talk her into putting the baby out for adoption, but the more time I spent with her, the more I grew to love the child she was carrying. Long before she had her baby, I knew that adoption was not an option. Neither did I succeed in my original hopes of convincing her, or Jimmy, that their relationship was wrong. When my little granddaughter was only two months old, my daughter moved in with my former husband.

"I argued with God about my need to forgive. 'It would be easy to forgive,' I said, 'if this had been another woman, someone other than my own daughter.' 'It would be easy to forgive,' I cried, 'if both parties had come to their senses and ended their relationship.' 'It would be easy to forgive,' I rationalized, 'if my daughter and this man were not now together.' 'But, God,' I always concluded, 'how can you ask me to forgive this? Even seventy times seven won't cover it!'

"At the same time, I knew that I was going to be Amy's mother and little Chelsea's 'nanna' forever. I had to find a way of dealing with the constant pain I felt.

"In counseling sessions, a precious woman of God counseled me to pray this prayer:

> *Father, in the name of Jesus, I choose to forgive.*
> *Holy Spirit, I ask You to come and heal the wound and pain from the betrayal and rejection I feel.*
> *Father, I give You the bitterness, anger, and resentment.*
> *I choose to forget the offense and not rehearse it in my mind or to anyone else.*

"As I prayed this prayer on a daily basis, God began to pour His healing grace into my life. New offenses didn't seem to penetrate into my heart the way they once had. I began to pray Psalm 139, especially verses 23 and 24: 'Search me, O God, and know my heart; try me, and know my anxieties. And see if there is any wicked way in me, and lead me in the way everlasting.'

"Still, there was to be more forgiveness required. One day as I was reading God's Word, I came across 2 Corinthians 2:5–8, which says, 'But if anyone has caused grief . . . you ought rather to forgive and comfort him, lest perhaps such a one be swallowed up with too much sorrow. Therefore I urge you to reaffirm your love to him.'

"To forgive from a distance, in the secret places of my heart, was one thing. To forgive verbally in a face-to-face encounter with the offending party—which I had done—was another. But to actually affirm my love for Amy and Jimmy and to bring comfort to them—that seemed to be asking too much. And yet here was God's Word. 'Now whom you forgive anything, I also forgive. For if indeed I have forgiven anything, I have forgiven that one for your sakes in the presence of Christ, lest Satan should take advantage of us' (2 Cor. 2:10–11).

"I thought of all who knew about this offense. I recalled how this incident had brought estrangement between my daughter and her brothers, and estrangement from our friends and loved ones. I wept. Only open affirmation and forgiveness could bring healing to *all* who had been hurt.

"The path to forgiveness, including this last step, has not been an easy one. It has taken five years for me to reach the point where I was reconciled to Amy, who now has a second child. I have been able to face the father of my daughter's children, once my husband, and confirm my love toward him as a brother in Christ. I also felt convicted in my prayer times that I needed to go back to my children's father, whom I had not seen in more than seventeen years, and confirm my forgiveness to him.

"Why forgive? Because the pain of *not* forgiving is intolerable. The destruction caused by offenses continues until forgiveness is given. And most important, I cannot be forgiven and move forward in my life until I forgive."

Jill was brought face-to-face with the fact that there's more to forgiving our enemies than simply saying in our hearts, "I forgive." Jesus gave us the full agenda for forgiveness when He said, "But I say to you who hear: Love your enemies, do good to those who hate you, bless those who curse you, and pray for those who spitefully use you" (Luke 6:27).

When a brother or sister in Christ offends us, we have no choice but to forgive. To be forgiven gives us the motivation to forgive, and to forgive is to put ourselves into the position where we can be forgiven. Forgiveness is cyclical, initiated by God, and never-ending. When enemies offend us, however, we are to go several steps further. We are to love them . . . do good to them . . . bless them . . . and pray for them!

What a tall order! Still, God would not require it of us if we were incapable, through Him, of doing it. Forgiveness is more than meets the eye. It is a radical change in our entire way of approaching people and trials. It is never what we would choose to do in our own human natures; *it is always what God chooses to do through us.*

The Process of Forgiveness

Forgiveness is a process. It's a process that takes time, often months or years. But time alone doesn't bring forgiveness. As Dr. Stanley writes in his book *Forgiveness,*

> Forgiveness is a much more involved issue than just putting time between us and the event or saying some words in a prayer. It is a process that involves understanding our own forgiveness and how that applies to those who have hurt us.
> Once we understand the depth of our sin and the distance it put between us and God, and once we get a glimpse of the sacrifice God

made to restore fellowship with us, we should not hesitate to get involved in the process of forgiveness. To understand what God did for us and then to refuse to forgive those who have wronged us is to be like the wicked, ungrateful slave Jesus described. . . . But the believer who will not forgive another is even more guilty and more ungrateful than that slave. The first step, then, is to realize that we have been totally forgiven of a debt we could never pay and thus have no grounds for refusing to forgive others.

Forgiveness must become a rhythm of life. That's why we pray daily, "Forgive us our sins as we forgive those who have sinned against us." On some days, you may need to pray this every hour!

Choose each day to forgive *before* you are sinned against. Set a pattern in your life to choose automatically to forgive rather than habitually hold grudges or harbor bitterness, anger, and resentment in yourself. Practice grace and forgiveness on a daily basis so that when you need to forgive a major offense, you will already be disciplined in these behaviors.

Gail McDonald in *Keep Climbing* notes, "Forgiveness is more often a life-style of grace than a one-time act."

Layers of Forgiveness

Many times we don't realize either the full extent of our own forgiveness by the Lord or the full extent to which we must forgive in one prayer session. Unforgiveness often is peeled away from its stranglehold on our hearts one layer at a time—layer after layer after layer.

This was true in Kimberly's life. She began at one point of forgiveness and ended up at one she didn't expect.

For eight years as a young child, Kimberly was sexually abused by her father. Through prayer, she released her father to the Lord and was able to forgive.

Other images and words of her father, however, kept haunting her. She remembered the time when she was twelve and had baked biscuits for supper. Jokingly, her father had picked one up and thrown it to the floor where it landed with a thud. He had said to Kimberly, "These biscuits are so hard and so heavy I just wanted to see if one would go all the way through the floor to the basement." Kimberly had been crushed in spirit.

At age sixteen, she took a job at the telephone company after school. The job ended at 10:00 P.M., and Kimberly had felt scared walking the two blocks to her car in the heart of her crime-riddled city. When she had shared her fears with her father, he had laughed and said, "Don't worry. If somebody grabs you, try to get under a bright light. When he sees what he's got, he'll let you go." Thirty years after the fact, Kimberly could still feel the sting of her father's words.

The time had come for Kimberly to forgive her father yet again— not for the physical, sexual assaults he had made on her body but for the verbal, emotional blows he had struck against her tender heart and her self-esteem.

Another layer of forgiveness. Still, there was more. When she heard a sermon based on Deuteronomy 5:16—"Honor your father and your mother, as the LORD your God has commanded you, that your days may be long, and that it may be well with you"— Kimberly's thoughts turned toward her mother. She uncovered deep resentment within her heart against a mother who had failed to rescue her or act on her behalf. Through much agonizing prayer, Kimberly eventually reached the place where she asked the Lord to soften her heart and show her what she could do to honor her mother and to release her fully in forgiveness to the Lord.

More forgiveness. And yet, there was still more. Kimberly next faced the fact that she had allowed her personal appearance to degenerate because she had never fully forgiven herself for her part in the sinful acts of her past—not that she had instigated those acts or been anything other than a victim—but that, even apart from her own will, she *had* been involved in sin.

Kimberly began forgiving the father who abused her physically. She ended a long journey of forgiveness by forgiving herself.

Forgiveness—no matter the person or the deed—must be forgiveness without strings. The other person's behavior may never change, as happened in Jill's case. It is God's job, not yours, to change lives. It is your responsibility to put yourself in a position where God can change *you!* At the same time, through forgiving, you put the other person into a position where God can act.

When you fail to forgive, you keep the offending party in a "cage" in your heart, as John and Paula Sanford teach. God has no access to the individual—to convict, punish, love, woo, compel, speak, act— until you unlock the cage in your heart and let the person go free!

How do you unlock this cage of unforgiveness and release the person to God?

First, speak from God's Word: *"Should I not have compassion on you, (person's name), even as Christ has had pity on me?"*

Next, say, *"I release you, _____, to the Lord. May His will concerning you be done in your life."*

His Will, Not Yours

It's important that you not insist on your will being done. God is not obligated to do your will toward the person; He is obligated only to accomplish His own will and purposes in the person's life, on His timetable, using whatever methods He chooses.

Finally, say aloud, *"You are free, _____, to go. I place you into the hands of Jesus. You are now His responsibility."*

You can trust God to act on your behalf when you forgive. Romans 8:28 promises that "all things work together for good to those who love God, to those who are the called according to His purposes." In choosing to forgive, you are acting on what God has called you to do. You can be assured He will take care of you. You do not need to bring about your own justice or revenge, just as you cannot bring about your own forgiveness.

Let God clear your name, restore your reputation, build you up, heal you, and bring good from bad. Trust Him to do it. That is His work, and His alone. No matter what you may say or do, or how clever and persuasive your arguments may be, you can never gain your own vindication as well as God can gain it on your behalf! Cry out to God as the psalmist did:

> Plead my cause, O Lord, with those who strive with me;
> Fight against those who fight against me.
> Take hold of shield and buckler,
> And stand up for my help.
> Also draw out the spear,
> And stop those who pursue me (Ps. 35:1–3).

The psalmist then went one step further: "Say to my soul, 'I am your salvation'" (Ps. 35:3). The psalmist *wanted* God to act on his behalf, and he wanted assurance in his heart that God *would* act. You can ask the same thing in prayer today!

You can also trust God to deal with the person who has offended you. In forgiving, you are casting the burden for that person on Him. Psalm 55:22 urges,

> Cast your burden on the LORD,
> And He shall sustain you;
> He shall never permit the righteous to be moved.

God alone knows how to carry the full burden of another person; He alone has the capacity to bear the weight of the sin. He alone is the Judge.

Romans 12:19 and Deuteronomy 32:35 have the same message: "'Vengeance is Mine, I will repay,' says the Lord." Our job is to forgive. God's job is to judge and to pass sentence. As long as we don't forgive, we're still judging. And God can't act as long as we hold the person tightly in our hands. Proverbs 24:17–18 says it this way:

> Do not rejoice when your enemy falls,
> And do not let your heart be glad when he stumbles;
> Lest the LORD see it, and it displease Him,
> And He turn away His wrath from him.

When we are gloating over our enemy's destruction, God will just let us gloat. He won't take action. We must release the person to the Lord. We must put the person in His hands to do with as He wills. That's truly the most awesome, powerful, and personally freeing thing we can do!

May our attitude be that of Job: "Indeed I have not allowed my mouth to sin by asking for a curse on his soul" (Job 31:30).

At the same time, we must recognize that God alone has the capability to redeem the offending person. We can count on His making every effort to do so, in love. God exacts justice, but it is a loving justice. The Bible promises us that *nothing* can separate the person from God's love, just as nothing can separate us from God's love. Romans 8:38–39 so declares: "Neither death nor life, nor angels nor principalities nor powers, nor things present nor things to come, nor height nor depth, nor any other created thing, shall be able to separate us from the love of God which is in Christ Jesus our Lord." That love has the capacity to cover all sins (see Prov. 10:12).

We must always come back to the point, however, that choosing to unlock the cage of our hearts and freeing another person—committing him or her into God's loving, just, and eternally capable hands—is a choice. We must choose to let go.

We must choose to be gracious. Proverbs 11:16 is one of my favorite verses in the entire Bible: "A gracious woman retains honor." When we deal graciously with others, in forgiveness, our own honor is retained. Proverbs 11:17 goes on to say, "The merciful man does good for his own soul, but he who is cruel troubles his own flesh." When we continue to harbor resentments and unforgiveness, we are actually doing ourselves physical harm. Our bitterness results in all kinds of ailments—psychological, physical, psychosomatic, demonization, you name them.

Several years ago Larry was preaching on the parable of Jesus about the unforgiving servant (see Matt. 18:23–35), and he made two important points. The first was that nobody can cast unforgiveness out of a person. A person must *choose* to forgive; it is an act of the will.

Larry's second point was related to these words of Jesus: "And his master was angry, and delivered him to the torturers [tormentors, KJV]. . . . So my heavenly Father also will do to you if each of you, from his heart, does not forgive his brother his trespasses" (Matt. 18:34–35). He observed that many people today are in torment of some kind—such as a physical or emotional sickness, a haunting memory, an addiction—because they have chosen NOT to forgive.

At the close of the service, Larry invited those who desired to forgive to come forward for prayer and as a sign of their commitment to forgive. As the people came forward, one woman was instantly healed of deafness in one ear. She could directly link the onset of her deafness with an action of someone close to her that she had chosen NOT to forgive. She had been in torment for years! Instantly, that torment was reversed when she opened the cage of her heart and let her unforgiven "prisoner" go free.

One day I was working in my garden, covered from head to toe with peat moss, when a neighbor approached me and commented that she was discouraged that she had not been able to quit smoking, no matter how hard she had tried. I asked her, "When did you *start* smoking?"

She said, "After I had a fight with my husband one time. I decided to take up smoking to spite him because I knew it was something he hated."

"Well, that's your answer," I replied. And there, on the sidewalk of our neighborhood, I prayed with this woman to be released in Jesus' name from the spirit of rebellion in her heart. She forgave her husband that afternoon, and instantly, she was freed from her bondage to nicotine! She has not smoked a cigarette since that day!

Are you in torment today? Can you remember when the torment began? Was it linked to an act of unforgiveness in your heart? Choose today to forgive.

More and more, physicians are realizing the link between bitterness and illness. Don't give them evidence to add to their statistics! Forgive, and do your soul and your body and mind a favor!

Self-Forgiveness

Perhaps the most difficult person to forgive is *not* the offender from the outside but the offender from within—the one you see in the mirror every morning! Standing in faith, believing that God has forgiven you when you repent and confess your sins to Him, you must take yet another step and forgive yourself. In this case, the offending party locked in the cage of your heart is yourself! Free that person, namely, you! Release yourself to the love and care of God, just as you would a second party.

Often, the inability to forgive yourself comes from a lack of understanding about what exactly Jesus accomplished on the cross. Recognize two things about God's forgiveness. First, it is total, complete, thorough, and all-encompassing. God doesn't just forgive part of your sin when you confess. He forgives your entire sin nature. He covers your sins completely with the blood of Jesus.

I recently counseled a woman who was having an extremely difficult time forgiving herself. She had become involved in an adulterous relationship, which she felt was mostly her fault. She had asked God's forgiveness, but she couldn't let go of the fact that she had sinned. In other words, she couldn't forgive herself, even after accepting by faith that God had forgiven her.

As we prayed together, I had a vision of this woman that I shared with her. I saw her holding the hand of Jesus but continuing to stare at her sins, abhorring the sight of them but unable to turn away. Then a waterfall of blood began to pour over a cliff above her. The flow of blood began as a trickle but soon became thicker and broader and more powerful until it created a wall of flowing blood between her and her sins. She could no longer see even the shadow of her sins behind the wall of blood; she could see only the blood that flowed between her and them.

When I shared this vision with her, this woman truly "saw" what God had done for her, and her bondage to the memory of her sin was broken completely!

What a wonderful vision that is for us to have for our own sins! The blood of Jesus is an ongoing, everflowing, eternally available sacrifice that completely covers our sins so that God no longer can see them. By His own promise and provision, God has declared that when He looks at us—His forgiven children—He sees only the blood of Jesus. What God no longer sees, we should no longer look for!

Second, God forgets when He forgives. Isaiah 43:25 declares what God does with our confessed sins: "I, even I, am He who blots out your transgressions for My own sake; and I will not remember your sins." Micah 7:19 says that God, in His compassion, casts "all our sins into the depths of the sea." Who are we to remind God of sins that He has already forgotten!

We must realize that when an offense comes against us, as God's beloved children, the offense is also against Jesus. It's impossible for someone to offend us without offending Him. Jesus taught that when we are persecuted for righteousness' sake—in other words, for doing God's work and will—we are to rejoice for we are in very good company! They persecuted the prophets in like manner. And like that of the prophets, our reward in heaven will be great!

Are you desperate today to be free of offenses? To rise above tribulation? To see God act fully on your behalf and restore your joy, your power, your confidence, your self-esteem, your reputation?

Then forgive those who offend you.

Forgive them daily.

Sow mercy.

Do good to them.

Bless them.

Pray for them.

And make the joyous discovery that when you freely forgive others, you will be freely and abundantly forgiven!

12 Desperate to Have a Way Out

"And do not lead us into temptation . . ."

The awful, never-ending process of combating temptation is God's
means of maturing us and conforming us to the image of
Christ. . . . To grow is to be tempted. We can't have one without
the other.

—*Charles Stanley*

We are all still in school.

No matter what age you may be, you are still being taught by God,
still being trained up into the full mature stature of Christ Jesus in
your inner person, still learning more about how to follow the Holy
Spirit's leading, still being prepared for graduation day when you pass
from this life into eternity. God is raising you up as a person with
whom Jesus will rule and reign this earth for a thousand years. For
that awesome responsibility, you must be prepared fully! God is
molding you—as a potter with fine clay—into a person with whom He
will live in heaven forever. For that joyous life ahead, you must be
freed of all sin's tarnish!

By academic training, I am a teacher. My foremost gift within the
body of Christ is that of teacher. As a teacher, I know the value of
tests. A test tells both student and teacher how much the student has
learned. If the student passes the test quickly and easily, the student is
ready to go on to more difficult, and often more personally meaningful, material. If the student fails the test, remedial work is necessary.
Many times, if the teacher can see that the student is eagerly learning
material, incorporating it into his or her thinking processes correctly,
applying it to life's situations appropriately, a test isn't necessary. It's

obvious to both student and teacher that the student is learning, and learning well. A test, then, comes at a point when the teacher questions, "How well is this student grasping the material?"

These same principles of learning and testing are true in our walk with the Lord. Tests will come, and we shouldn't be surprised when they do. The apostle Peter wrote,

> Beloved, do not think it strange concerning the fiery trial which is to try you, as though some strange thing happened to you; but rejoice to the extent that you partake of Christ's sufferings, that when His glory is revealed, you may also be glad with exceeding joy (1 Pet. 4:12–13).

In other words, don't be surprised when you are tested in your faith; rather, rejoice when you see that you have passed the test!

In James 1:2 we read, "Count it all joy when you fall into various trials." Joy? Yes, joy! Rejoice that you are being tested by God because He cares enough to train you up into maturity so that you will lack nothing and be complete in Him. God is in the process of conforming you into the image of His Son. We read in Romans 8:28–29, "And we know that all things work together for good to those who love God, to those who are the called according to His purpose. For whom He foreknew, He also predestined to be *conformed to the image of His Son* (emphasis added)."

This is not to say that God is the One who tempts us. The devil is the tempter, as Matthew 4:1–3 clearly tells us. James asserted, "Let no one say when he is tempted, 'I am tempted by God'; for God cannot be tempted by evil, nor does He Himself tempt anyone" (1:13). No, God is not the tempter, but He does allow temptation in our lives.

God's great desire, as our Master Teacher, is that we might be so attuned to His Holy Spirit that we can grow and develop without ever needing temptation. First Corinthians 11:31–32 states, "For if we would judge ourselves, we would not be judged. But when we are judged, we are chastened by the Lord, that we may not be condemned with the world." God's desire is that we would be able to test ourselves and never step off the path. Still, as human beings living on this earth, we must also face the fact that we have strayed from God's path, do stray, and will stray. Temptations will come.

There are other times when we are directly targeted by the devil as an objection for temptation.

That is the story of Job. The Bible tells us that Job was a righteous man, "blameless and upright, and one who feared God and shunned evil" (Job 1:1). Still, the day came when Satan said to the Lord, "Job only fears You because You have put a hedge around him and his household. You have blessed the work of his hands, and all his possessions have increased. But if You didn't bless him, he would curse You."

And the Lord responded to Satan, "Behold, all that he has is in your power; only do not lay a hand on his person" (Job 1:12). What faith the Lord had in Job! He trusted him to pass the test. He believed in Job to withstand any of the devil's assaults on his faith through attacks against his possessions, his family, and even his health. The Lord allowed the devil to have a season of temptation—all the way up to the point of near death—and when it was over and Job had passed with flying colors, God's reward was great. The Scriptures record, "Now the LORD blessed the latter days of Job more than his beginning." All of Job's losses were restored to twice the level he had before! (See Job 42.)

The temptation was for a season. The test ended. We are told in God's Word that at the beginning of Jesus' ministry, He was "led by the Spirit" into the wilderness where He was tempted by the devil for a season—a period of forty days. The temptation was but *for a season*. Most people I know spend their entire lives battling temptation, being led by it, beaten up by it, trapped into it, and desperate to escape it. That isn't God's plan! God's desire for us is to be led by the Spirit, taught by Him, our steps ordered in His Word.

I don't believe Jesus needed to be tempted for His own sake. Jesus was without sin, led continually by the Spirit, completely conformed into God's image. Why, then, was He led into the wilderness to be tempted? I believe it was to show *us* that *we can withstand temptation and how to do it by using God's Word*.

The Three Arenas of Temptation

Jesus was tempted at the same points that Adam and Eve and all human beings since them were tempted. He was tempted in these three areas: "lust of the flesh," "lust of the eyes," and the "pride of life."

"Lust of the flesh." Daytime and nighttime soap operas, jeans and suntan lotion commercials, tabloid newspapers—all present a steady message that sex without marriage is normal and desirable. The *fact* is that most marriage partners in America are faithful to each other, but you wouldn't know it from the media. Adultery, fornication, and even incest are regularly portrayed as the norm of our culture. Women casually enter into affairs and wonder why they suddenly feel trapped, guilty, ashamed, dirty. *Why, shame wasn't part of the original enticement!* Even Christian women and teenage girls are tempted to believe, "It's O.K. to have a sexual relationship with a man who isn't your husband as long as you love each other and are 'committed.' God doesn't care." Oh, God does care. That isn't His plan. We're being seduced by the tempter to give in to "lust of the flesh." And we're desperate to have a way out!

"Lust of the eyes." We're bombarded at every turn by images of things we're told we must have in order to live a successful life in this world. Commercials interrupt television and radio programming every few minutes and are now even placed before and after some movies and videos. Stores are arranged with a careful eye toward impulse buying and last-minute cash-register-stand purchases. The home shopping channels bring merchandise right into our homes for preview and sale—as easy as dialing a 1-800 telephone number and using a credit card. This is "in." You "must" have it. Call now while supply lasts.

We shop for pleasure and not for necessity. We are compelled with a hidden drive to find the latest bargain, even if we don't need anything. We've got to keep up with everyone else. We've got to show others how successful we are. We've got to have the "right stuff" in order to attract the "right people" into our lives. And as a result of giving in to the tempter, we find ourselves with closets and drawers and cupboards filled with things that we don't know how to use, don't have time to make, don't have occasion to wear, and don't really have a desire to own! So we have garage sales, and the shopping goes on.

We've fallen victim to the tempter who has played upon our "lust of the eyes." We struggle under a self-imposed deluge with things, desperate to find a way of paying for them and maintaining them at the same time. We're desperate to find a way out.

The "pride of life." Oh, this is a good one. It's one that is so insidious today because it often comes at us under the guise of self-esteem. We're being tempted continually as women to believe we can have it all, know it all, and be it all—in and of our own strength. Each of us is tempted to believe that she is somebody—someone of value and worth—because of what she accomplishes apart from God's love and a relationship with Him. That's a setup for the "pride of life" if there ever was one!

In buying in to these lines of temptation, women tend to fall into one of two categories. On the one hand, a woman says, "Well, I haven't done anything bad. I'm not a sinner. I don't need forgiveness. I don't need God." In so saying, she has just committed the sin of pride! Indeed, she has fallen short of the glory of God. To think otherwise is to put oneself on the same plane with God!

Another woman says, "Anything a man can do, I can do as well or better." She spends so much of her time and energy attempting to prove her equality that she misses the bigger issue. Our goal in life as women is not to become like men; it's to become like a Man, Jesus Christ, the only Son of God, who in Himself was the perfect reflection of our heavenly Father!

Trapped in our own self-righteousness or our own self-aggrandizement, we're desperate to have a way out of the constant pressure to be perfect, to be better, to be number one.

The lust of the flesh, the lust of the eyes, and the pride of life are not external to our lives. They are built-in drives within each of us. They are a part of who we are as human beings, the fallen daughters of Adam and Eve. They are the very traits that God is attempting to redeem, renew, regenerate, reform, and replace in our lives so that our only desire is for Him, His kingdom, and the doing of His will and purpose on this earth.

We must recognize that the devil doesn't hit us with a zinger from out of nowhere. Rather, he plays on those aspects of our fleshly nature that are already within us. As Charles Stanley writes in his book *Temptation,* "Temptation is not something we fall into; it is something we choose to give in to."

A bumper sticker I saw recently says it well: "Lead me not into temptation. I can find it myself."

The good news of the gospel is that we can overcome temptation. We don't *have* to give in to it; we can choose to withstand it. The real question is, "How?"

First, we must put on the spiritual armor that God has provided for us to withstand temptation. Ephesians 6:10–18 describes the defensive weapons we have at our disposal so that we "may be able to stand against the wiles of the devil" and "withstand in the evil day."

The Girdle of Truth

We women know about girdles, don't we? At least our mothers knew about them. Girdles hold us together, firm us up, keep us feeling stronger. In Ephesians, we are told to put on a girdle of truth. Knowing and speaking the truth provide the defense for us in our most vulnerable moments as women.

The King James Version says that this girdle of truth covers the "loins," the most secret part of a woman's body. We often try to hide our deepest hurts or our sins in the secret places of our hearts. It's God's desire that we let light—the light of truth—shine into those dark crevices of our souls.

People may accuse you of not knowing anything, but let me assure you, you can know the TRUTH. God has made that available to anyone who will diligently seek after it.

When Jesus was tempted by the devil in the wilderness, He didn't engage in a conversation with him or argue with him. He simply quoted back to him the TRUTH of God's Word. When the devil said, "Why not turn these stones into bread?" Jesus responded, "Man shall not live by bread alone, but by every word that proceeds from the mouth of God" (Matt. 4:4).

The devil tempted Jesus in this way after Jesus had fasted for forty days and nights. He was physically weak from physical hunger. Satan is merciless and will always attack us in our weakened condition and at our weakest point.

The devil says to women today, "God doesn't love you. If He really loved you, He wouldn't have let this bad thing happen to you. He would have prevented your poverty, your divorce, the death of your child. He'd do something to provide what you need." You see, the devil tries to get us to focus on our outward conditions, the material world, the external circumstances . . . our "lack of bread."

We defeat him when we say, "Devil, there's more than meets the eye here. The outer condition of my life isn't the whole story. There's an 'inside' story I'm going to tell you about, and it's this: no matter what may happen to me on the outside, I'm staying with God on the inside. Jesus Christ is my Truth, and He lives in me. No matter what may happen in the exterior, outer, material world around me, I choose to keep my spirit strong, singing the mighty praises of God and looking to Jesus as the Author and Finisher of my faith." That's the TRUTH! It's part of our arsenal of defensive weapons any time the devil tries to tempt us by getting our eyes off Jesus and on to our weakened condition.

The Breastplate of Righteousness

What does a breastplate of armor cover? All of the vital organs of the body: the heart, lungs, stomach, liver, and so forth—those organs necessary for sustaining life.

Righteousness—our position of right standing with God—comes when we accept the provision of Jesus' shed blood as the sacrifice for our sins. We trade in our righteousness for His. We no longer claim to be without sin, attempt to escape sin by our own cleverness, or reject God's plan. We repent of our sins, confess them to God, receive God's forgiveness, and take on the breastplate of His righteousness to cover our lives. Without God's forgiveness and the righteousness of Jesus covering our lives, we're vulnerable. We're subject to death. We have no protection for our hearts. With forgiveness, however, we're covered by His righteousness.

The devil comes to women today and says, "You've made another mistake. Wow, have you messed up! You really blew it this time. What a hopeless case! Can't you do anything right? You'll never amount to anything!"

Our defense is *not* to extol our own virtues or to tell the devil how bright, capable, and otherwise "together" we may be, at least most of the time. Our defense is to say, "Devil, I'm covered with the breastplate of righteousness, and furthermore, it's a designer breastplate. It was designed especially for me by my Creator. It bears the signature of Jesus Christ of Nazareth on it. Therefore, I'm protected from your lies. I don't stand in my own righteousness. I stand in His righteousness, and He has defeated you forever. You have no claim on my heart, my life, or anything vital to my life."

The Helmet of Salvation

One of the foremost fiery darts of the devil is to try to convince us that we are not forgiven. The devil will come again and again with subtle lies: "You know, you wouldn't be tempted if you were truly a Christian. You must not be saved. How do you know you're saved? If you were, you wouldn't have acted that way, would you?"

The devil attacks our minds to bring about doubt. That's why we need a *helmet*—it protects our minds!

Jesus faced this temptation in the wilderness when the devil said, "If You truly are the Son of God . . ." He was attempting to plant doubt. Jesus responded, "It is written again, 'You shall not tempt the Lord your God'"(Matt. 4:7). In other words, "Devil, you have no authority to countermand what God Himself has said about Me."

We defeat the devil when we say to him, "God says I am saved according to His Word. God says that he loves me, He has forgiven me, our relationship is intact, and He is living through me. You have no authority to change God's order of things in my life, to deny His promises, or to tear down what God has built up in my life."

The girdle of truth, the breastplate of righteousness, the helmet of salvation—these are our foremost defensive weapons against the devil's temptations. They are the answers to the test!

What happens if the temptation continues? Then we pull out of the depths of our will the power to endure. Ephesians 6:13 says, "And having done all, to stand."

We refuse to be moved. We refuse to give in. Having done and said everything we know to do, we choose to remain standing.

The Power to Endure

Jesus wasn't tempted just once. Or twice. He was tempted three times. The good news to us is that He didn't give in after the first temptation. Or the second. Or the third. He stood.

The Lord promises that when we make a stand in faith, He will empower us by the Holy Spirit to hold that stance. We must first declare our position; He then will enable us to hold it.

When we resist the devil, he must flee (see James 4:7). One of the foremost ways we resist the devil is to tell him that the time has come for him to go . . . now!

Jesus did this when the devil came a third time and tempted Jesus to bow down and worship him in order to gain the kingdoms of this world.

That's not an uncommon temptation to us today. The devil comes again and again and says, "If you'll just compromise in this area, your boss will give you that raise or promotion you want. If you'll just compromise in giving your tithe to the church, you'll have more money to spend on things you want. If you'll just compromise by not speaking up about the Lord, your friends will think more highly of you and invite you to more parties." All of that is the same as saying,

"If you'll just bow down and worship me and follow my commandments instead of worshiping God and following His way . . . I'll give you this world."

Jesus had an answer for the devil: "Away with you!" The King James Version says simply, "Begone!" Jesus commanded the devil to leave him, and as the devil departed, Jesus reminded him, "You shall worship the Lord your God, and Him only you shall serve" (Matt. 4:10).

We have been given that same authority to command the devil to leave our lives. We can say to him, "Get out of my life. Stop this temptation. Begone! I choose to worship the Lord God, and guess what, devil, that is ultimately what you are going to have to do, too!"

When we speak to the devil, we are giving voice to our resistance. Our resistance isn't a silent "underground" one. It's a bold, vocal one. It's a proclamation of our will into the heavenlies.

And what happens when we take action like this? God has promised that when we do the resisting, He will turn our resistance into a brick wall against which the devil has no hope. The devil must flee. At the same time, we get stronger. It's a double win!

The apostle Peter urges,

> Be sober, be vigilant; because your adversary the devil walks
> about like a roaring lion, seeking whom he may devour. Resist
> him, steadfast in the faith, knowing that the same sufferings are
> experienced by your brotherhood in the world. But may the God of
> all grace, who called us to His eternal glory in Christ Jesus, after
> you have suffered a while, perfect, establish, strengthen, and settle
> you (1 Pet. 5:8–10).

Our facing temptations and refusing to give in to them develop within us patience . . . endurance . . . strength to stand. Doing these things brings us to perfection . . . establishment . . . and a settling in our spirits about God, ourselves, and His kingdom on this earth. Our victory over temptation deepens our trust in God to be there with us when future fiery trials strike.

We should heed the words of James: "Count it all joy when you fall into various trials, knowing that the testing of your faith *produces patience. But let patience have its perfect work, that you may be perfect and complete, lacking nothing*" (1:2–4, emphasis added). Coming through trials and temptations changes us for the better.

Some time after the conversion of Augustine, he came face-to-face with the woman who had been his evil genius for many months, having dragged him deeper and deeper into the slavishness of sin until he had been freed from its bonds by the regenerating power of the Cross. When he would have passed her with only a formal nod, she stopped him and said, "Augustine, do you not know me any more? See, it is I." Looking at her a moment, and knowing that she no longer held him in her evil spell, Augustine replied, "But it is not I" (from *No Longer Augustine*).

The Reward for Withstanding Temptation

The reward for going through temptation is that we come out stronger on the other side. We grow. We gain spiritual power. We become more like Jesus. The eternal part of our being—our will to be more and more like Jesus—is reinforced, and a little more of the lust of the flesh, the lust of the eyes, and the pride of life is stripped away from us.

The apostle John wrote,

> For all that is in the world—the lust of the flesh, the lust of the eyes, and the pride of life—is not of the Father but is of the world. And the world is passing away, and the lust of it; but he who does the will of God abides forever (1 John 2:16–17).

Cling to that promise. When you resist temptation and overcome it by the power of the Holy Spirit, you are being prepared for an eternal future with the Lord. Your earthly, fleshly, pull-you-down nature is being chipped away. In its place, God is causing to grow within you His divine likeness.

Our victory over trials and temptations also *establishes* righteousness in us. "No chastening seems to be joyful for the present," the writer to the Hebrews said. "Nevertheless, afterward it yields the peaceable fruit of righteousness to those who have been trained by it" (Heb. 12:11). Just as physical exercise strengthens our muscles, so overcoming temptations and trials strengthens our souls.

After Jesus went through the temptations in the wilderness, "angels came and ministered to Him" (Matt. 4:11), and He "returned in the power of the Spirit" (Luke 4:14). That's God's promise to us, too. God will not leave us in a weakened position. He'll heal our wounds and strengthen our weaknesses by His Spirit. He'll turn our losses into triumphs. He'll reward us and empower us.

Are you desperate today to get out of a fiery trial or temptation?

Stay IN the Lord. Wrap yourself up in His truth, righteousness, and salvation. Seek God's peace. Resist the devil by standing in the Lord. Command him to flee from you.

Expect to come through your temptations. Expect to pass the test. Expect God to be faithful as you cling to Him and endure until the end.

James 1:12 affirms, "Blessed is the man who endures temptation; for when he has been approved, he will receive the crown of life which the Lord has promised to those who love Him."

Expect to be wearing a victor's crown!

13 Desperate to Be Safe

". . . But deliver us from the evil one."
(PART I)

He who makes God his refuge shall find him a refuge; he who
dwells in God shall find his dwelling protected.

—*Charles Spurgeon*

My friend Nona had a fierce hulk of a man break into her New
York City apartment one day while she was at home. Surprised to
find her there but intent on his purpose, he said, "Lady, I'm not going
to hurt you. I'm just going to rob you, and I won't hurt you if you
promise to stand over there and mind your own business."

Nona replied, "Buddy, you've got this all wrong. *I'm* going to hurt
you!"

The man didn't realize that the young woman facing him held a
black belt in karate. And so it was that the police found him begging
her for mercy when they arrived!

There are times when the devil isn't smart enough to know that he
is picking a fight with someone he can't defeat!

Have you seen the movie *The Bear*? In it, a mountain lion is stalk-
ing the young bear cub and nearly has him in his claws, but suddenly,
the mountain lion tucks his tail between his legs and slinks away. We
see the little bear cub standing on his hind legs, roaring in a comical
imitation of the truly fierce roar of a full-grown grizzly bear. Instinctively, we know that no mountain lion is going to be scared away by
his puny effort. Just as we are questioning, "Why?" the camera pulls
back to show us the whole scene. Several yards behind the little bear
cub is his friend and protector standing on his hind legs at gigantic
grizzly bear height, his front paws raised high, mouth open and men-
acing, eyes glaring. The mountain lion knows that in the face of this
new evidence, he's way out of his league!

Our stance in combating the devil in times of danger must be one of total reliance on a Source of power greater than ourselves and greater than the devil. That can only be Jesus Christ, the Son of the living God! If we try to take on the devil in our own strength and ability, we are a comic imitation of the real thing. We are laughable. But if we take him on in the strength of the Lord Jesus Christ, the One who has already bruised his head and won victory over him forever, the devil is out of his league!

Offenses come. Tribulation comes. Fiery trials come. It's always something. The real questions are, When do we fight? Whom do we fight against? When do we take an offensive posture rather than a defensive one?

The Devil Is a Usurper

We must recognize at the outset that the devil is a usurper of what is not properly his. He is a liar—in fact, the father of lies. He steals, kills, and destroys whenever, wherever, and whatever he can. That's his nature, as Jesus carefully outlined it in John 10:10. The devil wants everything that rightfully belongs to God, including you and me. He'll take whatever we give to him through sin, neglect, or ignorance.

When do we fight against the devil? All the time! We resist *all* of his efforts against us. We refuse to give in. We resolve not to give him an inch. In fighting the devil, we can't underestimate his resolve against us. His defeat is assured, but there's still deadly fight in him. He's mortally wounded, but as we know from watching animals, a mortally wounded creature is the one that lashes out with all the more intensity and extreme fury in a last-ditch effort to grab hold of life.

Don't laugh at the devil or take him lightly. He knows he's doomed, and he'd like nothing more than to go down taking you in his clutches. He is the enemy of your eternal soul, and he is seeking to devour you even today.

The Bible teaches, "Give no place to the devil" (see Eph. 4:27). That says to me that God considers it within our authority to claim portions of this earth as God's kingdom—to put our foot down in prayer and call out what is rightfully God's from the north, south, east, and west, and to hold that inheritance of God in safekeeping until the return of the Lord Jesus.

Furthermore, the devil has no legal right to rule over your life, family, or possessions unless you give it to him. God intends for you to keep what He has given you. He wants to see no soul led astray, no marriage destroyed, no child lost to evil. His desire is that you enjoy an ABUNDANT life, one filled to overflowing with meaning, purpose, and His good gifts—spiritual, material, and relational (family, friends, and loved ones in the church).

Many times, however, when trials and offenses come against us, we fail to see the devil at work. We misjudge his cleverness and his wily ability to use people for his purposes. The fight you have with your husband or boyfriend, the disagreement with your children that got out of hand, the struggle with your supervisor, the ongoing battle with the press to restore your reputation, the intense frustrations you feel in trying to convince the board to vote favorably on your behalf— all of these are not mere human issues. The apostle Paul plainly states, "We do not wrestle against flesh and blood, but against principalities, against powers, against the rulers of the darkness of this age, against spiritual hosts of wickedness in the heavenly places" (Eph. 6:12). Our battles are first and foremost spiritual ones.

Don't battle against the devil's pawns. Men and women who come against your stand for the Lord, and who persecute you for righteousness' sake, are merely operating according to directives from their master—the devil. Don't get your eyes on them and lose sight of your real enemy.

On the other hand, we must also be wise in recognizing that everything bad that happens to us is not the result of the devil. Sometimes we make mistakes and bring things on ourselves. We err; we goof; we trip and fall; we sometimes sin. We're human beings who don't have all the answers and who sometimes stumble blindly into problems. In those cases, we need to face up to our faults and ask forgiveness of God and others. We need to repent and trust God to restore to us what we have lost through our sin, neglect, or ignorance.

How can we tell the difference between a spiritual assault from the devil and the consequences of our own will or error?

The Nature of Spiritual Battles

First, hatred will abound. The attack against you will not be a simple slap in the face or an unkind word intended to set you back or put you down. The attack against you will be manifest with a fierce blind rage intended for your complete and absolute destruction forevermore. Your enemy doesn't simply want to punch you out; he wants to kill you. He doesn't want to steal a bit of your territory; he wants to rob you to the point that you have nothing left. He doesn't want to injure you slightly so you'll bow in defeat; he wants to destroy you so that you can never get up again.

Second, fear will abound. You'll find yourself locked into panic, feeling as if there's no place to turn and nothing you can do. The devil comes "like a roaring lion"—not a true lion but sounding like one (see 1 Pet. 5:8). The devil's roar is intended to cause fear to strike your spirit and immobilize you. That kind of fear will keep you from moving forward, taking risks of faith, and stepping out to speak the gospel message. When fear—that spiritually gripping fear, not a normal fear rooted in common sense—is overwhelming, you are in a spiritual battle.

You can always rest assured that God does not give you a spirit of fear. His appropriation for you is power, love, and a sound mind (see 2 Tim. 1:7).

Third, you will find you are able to think of nothing else. All thoughts will come back to the trial or temptation you are facing. You literally will not be able to think of anything else. Every spare moment will be spent fantasizing about what you would do "if only." As Francis Frangipane writes, "The territory of the uncrucified thought life is the beachhead of satanic assault in our lives. To defeat the devil we must be crucified in the place of the *skull*!"

Fourth, the issue will be magnified out of proportion long after forgiveness has taken place. The devil will take your mistakes and errors and blow them up to huge proportions, taunting and accusing you with their image, even after you have confessed and repented of your sins to God. When your thoughts continually return to sins that you have confessed to God and for which you have received forgiveness, you are in spiritual battle. God forgot your sins the microsecond after He forgave you. It is the *devil* who comes again and again to accuse you of what has been forgiven.

Thank God, He has given us a way of fighting and winning these spiritual battles!

Within the provisions of the "whole armor of God" in Ephesians 6:10–18 are two powerful weapons: shoes and a sword.

Gospel Shoes

Have you ever noticed how many more styles of shoes are available to women than to men? It seems to be a natural trait of women to enjoy pretty shoes and to need a closetful of them!

The Bible speaks of our wearing the shoes of the "preparation of the gospel of peace" (Eph. 6:15).

"Preparation" means that we have taken the gospel message into our lives in such a way that we are continually looking for practical ways to live it out or to "walk in the Spirit." We are ready and we are not ashamed, as the apostle Paul wrote, "For I am not ashamed of the gospel of Christ, for it is the power of God to salvation" (Rom. 1:16). The gospel has power in and of itself to change lives. IT is the power of God to salvation. Like a battery, Jesus, the Ever-Ready One, lives within us. He is always instant, in and out of season. Therefore, we can say with confidence, "I am ready, and I am not ashamed."

To be prepared in the gospel, you must know what your Bible says. Are you reading God's Word for yourself? Are you asking God to show you how to use His Word and how to apply it to your life on a daily basis? Or are you letting someone else tell you what God says? Read God's Word daily. Prepare yourself in it.

It's only when we prepare ourselves with God's Word that we have the ability to discern whether we should walk away from a situation or stand our ground. These shoes of the gospel are a little like those described in the old popular song: "These boots are made for walking." Our "gospel shoes" are made either for walking away from a fight, or for tromping all over the enemy. It's up to us to discern— through the Word of God and by the power of the Holy Spirit working in our lives—which course of action to take.

Consider the mother bird training her babies to leave the nest. The time has come for them to learn how to fly. As she kicks her babies out of the nest, she stays close by, occasionally flying under a struggling baby to lift it up and get it back on course. She teaches it to avoid the cat. She also teaches it, if necessary, to attack the cat, swooping down upon it, pecking at it, and causing it to run for cover.

That's the way the Lord tenderly teaches us. There's a time to fly away; there's a time to attack.

Only as we know the gospel in its fullness can we know when to flee and when to stand our ground and fight. And the number one criterion, the Scriptures say, is this: What will establish God's peace in this situation?

At times, getting into the fray—wading right into the thick of things—is necessary for us to truly be the blessed peacemakers that Jesus calls us to be. We may need to intervene, to make a stand for righteousness, to be a voice crying in a wilderness.

At other times, fleeing a situation may bring God's peace.

So many women today are being told that they must stick out a bad marriage, no matter how abusive it may be, in order to be in God's will. That may not be at all what will bring God's peace to all parties involved, including the abused woman! It's O.K. to flee—to separate, to get away from the abuse, to rush to a safe haven—in order to get well. We don't ask a wounded soldier to stay on the battlefield; no, we carry him to safety behind the lines, and when his wounds are healed and he is strong once again, we return him to battle. We don't ask a sick person to continue to perform all of her normal duties; no, we give her time and space to rest and recover. That's often what needs to happen in a bad marriage. A little time and distance may be necessary to restore peace, promote healing, and help a person recover strength in the Lord.

Don't stay in an abusive, unhealthful, or destructive situation of *any kind* unless God directly speaks to you and commands you to do so. Flee!

In the face of intense hatred and rage, speak a kind word and walk away.

Put some space between yourself and the abuser. It's not a crime to retreat. The war isn't over just because you've retreated to regroup your strength, get a new sense of direction, or reclaim God's peace. The war isn't over until you give up! And hear me carefully, retreating isn't giving up.

Consider the hawk—one of the most powerful birds of nature. When he is attacked by crows or kingbirds, he doesn't even bother to make a counterattack. He simply soars higher and higher in ever-widening circles until his tormentors leave him alone. He has not lost by retreating from their taunts; he has set himself on a higher plane!

Consider King David for a moment. He knew that he was God's chosen one; he had been anointed for the throne by the prophet Samuel long before he went to King Saul's court and married into Saul's family. He knew his rights "in the Lord." The Bible tells us that he was a man after God's own heart, quick to praise the Lord, quick to repent, quick to take a stand. After all, he had come into prominence by taking one of the most public stands possible for the Lord—facing Goliath in a high noon, one-on-one showdown!

David wasn't afraid of a fight. Still, when King Saul turned on him, narrowly missing him on more than one occasion with a flying javelin, David did not stand his ground and fight. He fled into the wilderness of En Gedi, and there he huddled in a cave waiting God's appropriate time for action. David did not declare war on the king; in fact, he declared mercy, refusing to kill Saul even when he had a prime opportunity. David did not encourage others to riot or over-throw the throne on his behalf. No, he held his peace from a distance, doing what he could to bring deliverance to his people, far away from the throne he was destined to occupy.

There is a time to flee. There is a time to stand. Again, you can know which to pursue only if you are taking the FULLNESS of the gospel into your own life and applying it regularly to situations you face on a daily basis. Ask the Lord when you read the Bible, "Please show me what this means to ME. Show me how to use this in MY life. Give me Your direction for what I am to do TODAY."

Above all, when you are faced with a temptation, ask the Lord, "How would You have me handle this so that it brings the greatest peace—Your peace, not just a lack of a squabble? Show me how to be a peacemaker!"

The Sword of the Spirit

Our arsenal of spiritual weapons has one weapon obviously in-tended for hand-to-hand combat with the devil. It is an offensive weapon as well as a defensive one. It is the sword of the Spirit—the Word of God.

This weapon is designed exclusively for use against the devil, not people. Some of us are very good at carving up our human enemies, putting our initials all over them. That isn't the purpose of God's Word. The sword of the Spirit is to be used for destroying evil spirits, not damaging human ones.

In our dealing with people, the sword of the Spirit becomes the "balm of Gilead." Our words from the Bible to those around us are always to be words of encouragement that forgive, build up, heal, bless, and restore.

We use the Word of God defensively when the devil comes to us and puts a lock on our minds by feeding us a lie about who we are, why we are here, or where we are going.

The Devil's Three Main Lies

The number one lie of the devil is this: "You aren't worth anything. Why would God love you? In fact, you've sinned so bad, how could God love you? You can't be saved."

We answer that lie by wielding our sword and quoting to the devil the Word of God, "Devil, listen up! God says He 'so loved the world that He gave His only begotten Son, that whoever believes in Him should not perish but have everlasting life' (John 3:16). Well, I'm 'whoever,' devil. I believe in Him, and therefore, I qualify!"

Find Scriptures on which you can base your identity. Know who you are in the Lord! God's Word provides a mirror in which you can see yourself as God sees you.

Memorize Scriptures that talk about your identity in Christ Jesus. Use them against the devil! They are a sword in your hand against the fear and an attitude of defeatism, discouragement, and bad self-image that he'd like to lay on you. Boldly declare to the devil: "I am a child of God. Jesus Christ died for me, and by my acceptance of His sacrifice, I am saved, cleansed from my past, given a future, and established for His purposes. I am in the process of being refined as pure gold. I have the hope of glory. I am God's righteousness on this earth. I am His witness to the lost. I am a vessel He has created and through which He works."

You can wear out the devil telling him who you are in Christ Jesus! Believe me, he won't stand around and listen to you for very long!

A second lie of the devil is this: "You don't deserve to be alive. You're just using up oxygen and occupying space. You're not worth anything. Why, you don't even have a job. You aren't producing anything. You aren't doing anybody any good." The devil will do whatever he can to convince you that you don't have a purpose in this life and that you should just roll over and play dead or, even better in *his* eyes, give up and kill yourself.

Stand against that lie with the Word of God! Wield your sword! Declare that in Christ Jesus you do have a purpose! Say, "I am here, devil, to establish the kingdom of God. That's my purpose. I do that first and foremost through prayer. My prayers count, and God honors my faithfulness in praying, for it is through the faithful prayers of His saints that God is given permission to do His work on this earth in the will and hearts of men. I extend His kingdom by raising up godly seed—by witnessing to those around me, either planting the good news of the gospel or watering it, cultivating it, or harvesting souls. If nothing more, I am a fountain of praise on this earth that cannot be silenced. I will bless the name of the Lord daily and voice His praises to the heavens. I will occupy until He comes or until He calls me to be with Him. That's my purpose!"

The third main lie of the devil is this: "You have no future. There's nothing more for you. There's nothing after you die."

If the devil can't intimidate you with fear, he'll try to discourage you by robbing you of hope. He's a thief. Never forget it. He delights in stealing hope!

Use the Word against him. Wield your sword by saying, "Devil, I'm bound for glory. Heaven is already my true home; I'm just not living there yet. I'm destined to rule and reign on this earth with Jesus for a thousand years, and after that, I'm residing with God forever in His heavenly kingdom. I'm destined to live wherever He is. A future is one thing I have, devil, that you don't have!"

Sometimes the devil will try to convince you that there's no future miracle in store for you on this earth. He whispers to you, "Your marriage will never work out. Your sickness will never be cured. Your runaway child will never return home. You'll never be able to do this thing that God has called you to do. Your witness for Christ isn't going to last."

Wield your sword. Declare to him, "Even though you slay me, yet will I serve Him. No matter what happens to me or around me, I will choose to love God. I will choose to stand on His promises for me. I will choose life. I will abide by His commandments and live my life according to His judgments, not yours, devil. I will believe for God's miracles, and I will not give up!"

Going on the Offensive

At other times in our lives, we are called by God to go on the offensive in praying and in wielding the sword of the Spirit.

A number of years ago I made a declaration to the devil, "The harder you make it on me, the harder I'm going to make it on you."

I came to that decision after experiencing a trend in our family. It seemed that every time Larry walked out the door of our home to go preach somewhere, sickness walked in.

It was almost like clockwork. Within two hours of Larry's leaving, somebody would come down with something major. It wouldn't just be a headache; it would be the headache of the century. Often it was Jo Anna who was stricken. She has had asthma all her life, and it seemed that most of her major attacks happened when Larry was away.

I got to the point that I was so depressed about this recurring situation—feeling sorry for myself with three young children and nowhere to turn and nobody to help carry the load—that I dreaded Larry's leaving. I'd brace myself as I kissed him good-bye, saying to myself, *Well, there he goes, and oh, God, here it comes again.*

Once after Larry left, I was awakened at two o'clock in the morning by Joy, our younger daughter, who said, "Mama, Jo Anna can't breathe." Well, there we were, in the middle of the night, and being a pastor's wife and knowing what it's like to be awakened at all hours, I decided not to call the doctor right away. I took Jo Anna into the bathroom and turned on the shower to create steam. I rubbed Vicks all over her chest. Nothing worked. Jo Anna still moaned in my arms, "I can't breathe, Mom."

What do you do? Well, I got mad. I said, "I have had enough of this. I have had all I'm going to take. I know what's going on here. It's all suddenly very apparent to me, and I'm tired of it. Devil, you've been beating me down and depressing me, ruining my days, spending our money on doctors, wasting my time. It's you that's behind making my kids ache and hurt and get sick all the time. Well, I'm sick of *you*, you lying, stealing, destroying devil. And I know what to do about it!"

Immediately I went to John Aaron's room and awoke him. Then I scooped up Joy, and the three of us went into Jo Anna's room and climbed up on her bed with her. I said, "Look here, kids. We can just lie down and play dead and let the devil run over us every time your daddy leaves. But I'm tired of doing that, and I've decided we're not going to live this way anymore."

They said, "Yeah, that's right, Mom! Let's fight back!"

I said, "We're going to take the Word of the Lord and start slashing at the devil with it. Now the Word of the Lord says that God's desire is that we prosper and be in health even as our souls are prospering. (See 3 John 2.) Well, our souls are prospering. So it's God's desire that we be in health, too. It's His will we're healed. Furthermore, Jesus got all beat up just so we could be healed, so let's pray and take hold of this thing."

And there we were at three o'clock in the morning, my three young children and I, assaulting heaven with our prayers and speaking to the devil, "We rebuke you, devil! You aren't going to have this family or steal our health. We're coming against you in the name of the Lord and this is what God has to say about you. . . ."

I stopped and listened to my children pray, and I thought, *The devil really overstepped his bounds this time. Not only does he have me on his case, but here are three young prayer warriors ready to take him on in case I miss something!*

In speaking to women all across this nation, I've discovered that one of the devil's favorite times to launch an assault is Sunday morning. He'll do just about anything imaginable to keep us out of the house of God and away from the anointed preaching of God's Word. That was once true in our house, too. The children would be well all week but would awaken ill on Sunday morning. Somebody would get depressed or upset about something that he never thought twice about Monday through Saturday. We'd sleep like babies all week but stare at the ceiling Saturday night and then miss the alarm.

When I get up on Sunday mornings now, I get up with both prayer guns blazing. I say, "You just wait, devil, until I get to church. I'm going to lay hands on everything that moves. I'm going to speak the Word of God. I'm going to sing praises to God as loud as I can sing. I'm going to see people healed and delivered and changed by the power of the gospel this morning."

Yes, the harder the devil tries to make it for me, the harder I'm determined to make it on him!

No Cowards

When Jesus taught us to pray, "But deliver us from the evil one," He never intended for us to be cowardly Christians. Whether we flee in order to get to a place of safety and strength from which we can launch an assault, or whether we stand and fight with sword shining . . . we are called to boldness. We are called to go from strength to strength and glory to glory—not to whimper and shrink away from the devil's roar.

We have God's assurance that when we make a stand and lift up the name of the Lord, He will send His angels to have charge over us. In fact, He'll send as many angels as are required for the task of guarding us in all our ways as we walk according to His will. Our security is God's priority! (We need to recognize, conversely, that His promise of protection doesn't extend to our doing things that are out of His will.)

Charles Spurgeon wrote,

> The Almighty is where His shadow is, and hence those who dwell in His secret place are shielded by Himself. What a shade in the

day of noxious heat! What a refuge in the hour of deadly storm! Communion with God is safety. The more closely we cling to our Almighty Father the more confident may we be.

Are the fiery trials heating up? Are the offenses increasing in intensity?

Stand in Jesus! You can rest assured that you'll be standing on the Rock that doesn't roll, hidden in the safe cleft of God's presence. There's no more secure place on earth!

14 Desperate to Be Needed

". . . But deliver us from the evil one."
(PART II)

He will have need to pray, he will be led to pray aright, and the answer will surely come. Saints are first called of God, and they then call upon God; such calls as theirs always obtain answers. Not without prayer will the blessing come to the most favoured but by means of prayer they shall receive all good things.

—Charles Spurgeon

I believe the greatest thing we can experience in life, other than love, is purpose.

Apart from purpose, people don't have a reason to live. They wander aimlessly, their days having no meaning. But God created each man and woman with a plan and purpose in mind. We were not accidents, regardless of the circumstances of our parents at the time of our conception. God intended for us to be here, for our lives to be full of meaning and purpose, and for us to contribute to the advancement of His kingdom on this planet.

Many of us, however, are looking for the one BIG event that will justify our existence, the one outstanding, noteworthy deed done for the glory of God. We're looking for the big moment when the spotlight falls on us and history is changed because we lived! Those moments rarely come for the vast majority of people.

Our purpose is *not* rooted in a once-in-a-lifetime major accomplishment or moment of recognition. Our purpose is greater than that! Rather, throughout our life span, we can affect *countless* numbers of individuals through making a wise decision here, offering an encouraging word there, living a life in which Jesus is allowed to once again walk the earth—only this time, in *our* bodies!

When we look at many of the famous men and women in the Bible, we tend to see only the one major feat that made them famous rather than the life that prepared them for that moment.

Consider Deborah. She was a judge of Israel, holding court under the palm tree outside her home. For years before she became a judge, she was called a "mother of Israel," a woman who learned through raising her family how to be a judge! The Scripture teaches that only those who have ruled their families well can have the insight to rule the household of God. When Barak faced the prospects of going to war against the mighty General Sisera, whom did he call? Deborah. She wasn't picked out of the clear blue sky. No, Barak went to Deborah because she already had a proven track record—a lifestyle—of being a wise and just arbitrator, a righteous woman who knew the plans and purposes of God!

And then there's Jael, another woman closely associated with the story of Deborah and Barak. Jael is the one who enticed the wicked Sisera into her tent, and when in utter exhaustion he had fallen into a deep sleep, she drove a tent peg through his skull. Jael had years and years of experience as a nomadic woman, setting her tents by driving tent pegs into the earth. She was prepared for the moment—both physically and spiritually—because of all the years that had gone before in seemingly uneventful, yet purposeful living.

Esther, perhaps the most famous queen of the Old Testament, did not become queen overnight. She had undergone months of careful preparation in beauty treatments and training in order to gain the poise and bearing that captured the king's heart. She had years of training in her uncle's household that gave her the inner fortitude to take a stand for righteousness and, through that stand, to see the deliverance of her people.

The fact that Mary was a virgin, willing to do God's will as a young teenager, was not an accident of the moment. Obviously, Mary's heart had been turned toward God at an early age; she had developed a "yes" attitude toward the will of God. Her entire lifestyle was one of purity and consecration. Consequently, when confronted with new and unusual circumstances in the will of God, she did not balk but willingly submitted herself to His purposes.

None of these women burst onto the scene as an "unknown, overnight wonder." God saw their lives, the purposeful way in which they had followed His leading and obeyed His commandments day in and day out. He did not give them a purpose because they just happened to be standing nearby. They were chosen for specific tasks because they had already steeped themselves in the ordinary day-to-day purposes of God!

A Purposeful Life-Style

Jesus used many examples in teaching us what our purposeful lifestyle is to be like. He said that we are to be:

Yeast—to raise up the level of faith, hope, and love among those around us.

Light—to glow so brightly in the darkness around us that others will follow us to the Lord.

Salt—to season the world and to make it thirsty for the Living Water who is our Lord Jesus Christ.

Jesus also said that we are to be:

Kings—to rule wisely and justly over our individual sphere of influence, to bear authority in this earth over spiritual matters, and to feel a responsibility for this earth and its people before God.

Priests—to intercede on behalf of our families and loved ones, to thoughtfully train those for whom we're responsible in the Lord, and to be godly examples to everyone who sees our lives.

Prophets—to tell others the good news of the gospel and point the way toward heaven.

What is your purpose today? Why is your life necessary for the God-designed scheme of things? You are to *be* salt, yeast, light, and a prophet, priest, and king in your world!

So much of our world today is caught up in DOING. In fact, one of the first things we ask someone we meet is, "What do you do?" We build résumés based on what we have done. We are a task-oriented goal-bound society. And yet, Jesus did not want us to spend our lives striving and competing to be human DOINGS. He needs us to be human BEINGS. He tells us that our purpose is *not* in DOING something grandiose nearly as much as it is in BEING persons who bear His purposes in our earthen vessels, living out our daily lives to His glory, carrying His presence wherever we walk, exhibiting His love whenever we speak, and showing forth His power in every area of need we enter.

A purposeful life-style may or may not result in a "big moment" in the history of the world, although it most certainly will prepare us for one should God so choose. (If a big moment does come, we must understand that it comes at God's instigation, not because we have manufactured it in our own strength or by our own cleverness.) But a purposeful life-style *will* most assuredly prepare us for eternity.

Yes, the *real* purpose of your life is to become a colaborer with God, to help Him effectuate His purposes here on earth. He does not arbitrarily do this. He chooses to work through you.

Righteous Seed

One day while in prayer, I had a wonderful vision of my family. We were all standing before the throne of God, and I was presenting each of our children to the Lord. Each one had received Jesus and had genuinely loved Him and joyfully served Him while here on earth. And then, in the next moment, each one of us heard, "Well done! Good and faithful servant!" What a moment!

My life's purpose is to accomplish this goal—to raise up righteous seed upon this earth. The righteous carry on the work of God, speaking His words and showing forth His glory from generation to generation. Remember the genealogies in the Old and New Testaments (that is, "so-and-so begat so-and-so, and they begat so-and-so")? Through the genealogies we see how one generation tells the mighty deeds of God to the next, causing His words, His truth, to endure to all generations.

Each generation, of course, has a choice about what it will do with the Word of God. Whatever those sons and daughters choose directly affects the quality of life both they and those around them enjoy. Again and again we read in the history of Israel that kings arose who followed after the ways of their fathers and mothers, for good or for evil. What a great obligation that places upon us as parents today! Perhaps no greater purpose is before us than to raise up sons and daughters who will follow after us . . . for the purpose of *good*. Righteous seed produces a righteous harvest!

You need not bear physical children to have this purpose of raising up righteous seed. As Christians, we are all called to raise up righteous seed in the spiritual realm. In fact, long before Eve bore her first son, Adam gave her a name that means, literally, "mother of all living." Eve was created with a mothering instinct—a desire to nurture and train and develop and love. Alice Painter, a Bible teacher in Colorado, points out in her teaching that a woman *"will* mother something." It may not be a child; it may be a husband, a boss, her dog or cat, and so forth. Our instinct, especially as women, is to raise up children—both physically and spiritually.

We must come to an understanding that the raising up of righteous seed is important work before God. In fact, nothing is more important! It's His heart's desire to see men and women brought into a saving knowledge of Him and a personal relationship with Him. It's His heart's desire to see boys and girls and men and women "grow up" in Christ Jesus—something that only happens as they are led and taught by their older brothers and sisters in Christ. It's His heart's desire to see righteousness spread across the earth as the gospel is extended, His kingdom is expanded, and His power is manifested.

From my early childhood, I've had the knowledge that my life was important, and that it was supposed to count for something. Much of that feeling of destiny, no doubt, has to do with the prayers of my parents. My mother and father had to wait ten years before they could be married; they fell in love during the Great Depression, and they both had families they had to help support financially. All during that time, however, they prayed and believed that when they did marry, they would have a child and their child would be either a pastor or a pastor's wife.

After Mama and Daddy were married, ten more years passed before I was born. Then, it was twenty more years before I brought Larry home to them so that he could talk with Daddy about marrying me. In all, Mama and Daddy prayed for forty years that their child would be "godly offspring," a righteous seed on this earth.

You may not have had parents who prayed for you that way. You may not have a sense of importance or destiny about your life. If that's the case, then let me share with you the good news: "You are vitally important to God. He has raised you up to be His righteousness on the earth and to reproduce yourself in godly seed. That's your purpose. Your life is extremely important to God and to His kingdom!"

Susanna was a woman who knew that she was called to raise up righteous seed. She knew that her life counted for God and that the lives of her children were of critical importance to Him. Susanna's husband, Samuel, was a traveling preacher who often left her at home with their children—nineteen of them over the years! Susanna made prayer an integral part of every day. (She had to; she didn't have Extra-Strength Tylenol!) Her children would later recall that when their mother retreated to a corner of their kitchen and put her apron over her head, she was *not* to be disturbed. That was her signal to her entire family that she was praying.

On Sunday evenings, Susanna held a Bible study for her children and their friends and family. Gradually, friends, neighbors, and church members asked to attend. Meeting in their own home in the early years of the eighteenth century, Susanna would lead the meeting by reading a sermon, praying, and then talking individually with those who had come. As the months passed, more and more people began coming to her Sunday evening Bible studies. The group that began with thirty people mushroomed to more than two hundred and become the spiritual strength of the church that her husband pastored.

Two of Susanna's sons are credited with launching a revival that kept England from the ravages of rebellion and civil revolution that had swept through France. Their names? Charles and John Wesley. In fact, the Methodist movement that Charles and John Wesley founded is given credit by many church historians as laying the foundation for the holiness movement in America at the turn of the twentieth century, a movement that gave rise to the charismatic movement in the church today!

Can one woman make a difference? Can one woman who catches sight of her mission to raise up righteous seed change the world—not through a grand movement but through a purposeful life-style? The answer must be a resounding yes!

It is in prayer that we sow the seeds of righteousness on this earth. Critical to your role as the "mother" of godly offspring is your call to pray.

Prayer—a Vital Part of Your Purpose

A number of years ago, I had a vision of myself having a conversation with the Lord in heaven. He said, "The time is short. I need warriors in the earth—men and women of renown who will do My will." Then I saw the Lord fashioning Larry, then me, and then our children, and then other men and women all over the world into warriors!

Another time, as I was preparing to teach this very subject to a group of women, I heard the Holy Spirit repeatedly say, "Come up higher! Come up higher!"

God wants *you* to come up higher! He wants you to see your life from *His* perspective—to rise above your mundane thoughts of yourself and see yourself from His vantage point and see your vital role in the kingdom of God.

God is calling men and women everywhere to become prayer warriors. Even as I write, Larry and I are preparing for a major expansion of our international ministry to take the message of prayer to the nations.

God needs *you* to be a prayer warrior. Why?

Because this world is in danger of destruction. God cannot tolerate sin, and our world is full of it. That has been the message of all of the great prophets of God, including those who walk the earth today. In Isaiah 59:15–16 we read these mournful words:

> Then the LORD saw it, and it displeased Him
> That there was no justice.
> He saw that there was no man,
> And wondered that there was no intercessor.

Ezekiel 22:30–31 tells us what happens when there is no one to stand in prayer:

> "So I sought for a man among them who would make a wall, and stand in the gap before Me on behalf of the land, that I should not destroy it; but I found no one. Therefore I have poured out My indignation on them; I have consumed them with the fire of My wrath; and I have recompensed their deeds on their own heads," says the Lord GOD.

Our job today is to make a wall—to build a hedge of protection around God's saints—and to stand in the gap before the Lord on behalf of those who are lost. Like the little Dutch boy who is credited with saving his nation because he stuck his finger in a leaking dike, we are called today to stand in the gaps that we see, to plug up the spiritual holes before us with our prayers. We may not be able to see the whole of this earth's need. In fact, if we could see it, we would probably be so overwhelmed that we'd be immobilized at the awesome size of the task. We are called to pray only for those needs that we see and know—the needs of our own lives, our family, our loved ones, our fellow church members, our beloved friends, those who minister the Word of God to us, our national leaders. No calling is higher than the call to pray, to stand in the gap before us, and to become spiritual warriors on this earth.

God Waits for Us to Pray

Everything that God does on this earth is in response to prayer. In other words, God will not act unless someone prays. Why is this so?

Because God gave man free will. God gave man a choice as to whether he wanted Him in or out of his life; God will not violate the free will He has bestowed. He waits for us to invite Him into situations, into lives, into cities, into nations. He waits until we cry out to Him for intervention, even though His heart is eternally longing to rescue, deliver, save, heal, and restore. We must ask before He will act.

Jesus looked straight into the face of a blind man named Bartimaeus and asked him, "What do you want Me to do for you?" (Mark 11:51). Jesus could see that Bartimaeus was blind. He was dressed like a blind man and acted like a blind man. When Jesus looked into his eyes, He could see without question that the man was blind. Yet, Jesus, because of God's law of free will, asked, "Bartimaeus, what is it you want Me to do for you?" When Bartimaeus said, "Lord, that I might receive my sight," it was then, and only then, that Jesus healed him.

Our prayers give God permission to work. They establish us as colaborers with God.

Maintaining Prayers

You are called to pray, first and foremost, "maintaining prayers." This is prayer that keeps an awareness of God's presence strong within you on a daily basis. Discipline yourself to pray the Lord's Prayer every day.

Daily prayer keeps your spiritual "pipes" from becoming corroded or blocked; it unstops your spiritual arteries so that the life of Jesus can flow through you freely.

Cover your family daily in prayer. As you're driving to work, ironing shirts, making beds, going for walks, nursing the baby, changing diapers, or working in the garden, pray for your loved ones.

Seek out the promises of God for each particular situation and person in your life, and declare those promises daily. Ask the Lord to give you a revelation about each person you love so that you can pray more effectively.

We live in a time when information is multiplying at a rate faster than any of us can comprehend. Are you aware that more than sixteen thousand medical journals will be published this year in America alone? There's that much new information in the world of medicine in just one year! Yesterday's information is old information; yesterday's

153

news is old news. The Bible, however, provides ETERNAL TRUTH, not news. Truth doesn't change. When you grab hold of it for your life, it changes not. And when you find Scriptures that pertain to you and your loved ones, you can count on the fact that God's Word is the same yesterday, today, and forever. His promise to you is not given today and taken back tomorrow. It abides. It remains.

When we sow God's Word into our lives and into the lives of our loved ones on a daily basis, we are sowing truth that bears righteous fruit, lasting fruit, eternal fruit. It's always good. It benefits all of our lives. It lasts into eternity.

Find Scriptures that relate to yourself, for example, "Open my eyes, that I may see wondrous things from Your law" (Ps. 119:18). Begin to pray, "Open my eyes, Lord. Help me to see all that You want me to see today. Show me what I need to see in order to do Your will. Don't let me focus on the negative. Let me take delight in the 'wondrous things.' As I read Your Word, open my spiritual eyes to see You, rising up from the pages."

Matthew 6:22–23 states that "the lamp of the body is the eye. If therefore your eye is good, your whole body will be full of light. But if your eye is bad, your whole body will be full of darkness. If therefore the light that is in you is darkness, how great is that darkness!" Pray, "Lord, I want a single eye, one that is focused on You, not looking to the right or left. I want to see your truth as I walk through this day. Dispel the darkness in my life, O God. Don't let anything sinful reside in me. Search my heart and show me the things for which I need to repent and be forgiven!"

Second Corinthians 4:4 declares, "Whose minds the god of this age has blinded, who do not believe, lest the light of the gospel of the glory of Christ, who is the image of God, should shine on them." Pray, "Oh, Lord, don't let the god of this world blind me and keep me from believing for all that You want to give to me and cause me to become. Shine the light of the gospel into my life. Remove the blinders. Help me to see clearly the face of Jesus. Help me, as I behold Him, to desire to be transformed into His image. My heart's desire is that when others look at me, they'll see You!"

I suggest you make a notebook of Scriptures that speak to you about yourself and your loved ones. As you read God's Word daily, make entries in your notebook. Write out the verses. And then consult your notebook daily in prayer.

You may have an entire section of Scriptures for your husband. Psalm 1:1–3 is the first entry I suggest you make:

Blessed is the man
  who does not walk in the counsel of the wicked
or stand in the way of sinners
  or sit in the seat of mockers.
But his delight is in the law of the LORD,
  and on his law he meditates day and night.
He is like a tree planted by streams of water,
  which yields its fruit in season
and whose leaf does not wither (NIV).

Do you see how you can pray that daily for your husband? "O God, I pray that You will not let my husband be adversely affected today through contact with those who are wicked. Don't let him heed the counsel of those who mock Your Word. On the contrary, help him love and hunger for Your Word. Let him bring forth fruit. Don't let him be discouraged or wither in the heat of the battle."

Add Proverbs 25:5—"Remove the wicked from his presence that he can be established in righteousness—and Psalm 142:7—"Then the righteous will gather around me"—to your prayer. Pray, "O Lord, put righteous people all around my husband today. Let them share Your wisdom with him and teach him more about You."

Find verses for your children—each one of them.

Psalm 127:3 teaches that "children are a heritage from the LORD." Pray, "I thank You, Lord, that You have given me my children and that they are a gift from You. Help me always to value them as Your blessed gift to me."

From 2 Timothy you learn this: "For God has not given us a spirit of fear, but of power and of love and of a sound mind" (1:7). Pray, "Heavenly Father, I pray for my child today that You will drive fear far away from him. Fill him with power from You. Let him feel Your love and show Your love to others. Give him a sound mind to learn everything he needs to learn in school and in life today."

Ask the Lord to reveal to you a special set of Scriptures for each child—verses that pertain to special gifts, the unique personality, and God's specific call on the child's life.

For family members, friends, ministers, and persons "out of the blue" for whom you have a special burden, ask the Lord to give you specific Scriptures for them. Ask Him to reveal to you how to pray for your pastor, your Sunday school teacher, and those in your church who are in ministry or in need.

Pray daily. Maintain your presence in the gap. Tend the hedge of protection that you have established!

Prayers of Agreement

There are times and situations when praying by yourself is not enough, when you need spiritual reinforcements. Then you need to come into agreement with other believers. The Bible says that in our role as warriors, each of us will put one thousand to flight, but when two of us stand together, we'll put *ten* thousand to flight (see Deut. 32:30)!

Sometimes the spiritual warfare is so intense, the opposing forces so entrenched, that it is necessary for us to "bring in the big guns." That's when you need the power of the prayer of agreement. Your prayer partners may be believing members of your own household. Do not discount your young children. Their faith is so pure, they make formidable foes to the enemy, and these times provide great opportunities to train them to become warriors.

You may also join with other godly women. Barbara Grisell, who was the women's ministry director at the Church on the Rock for many years, once said to me about the weekly prayer group that she led, "Everything we ever really prayed for happened." What a testimony to the power of prayer!

We saw a powerful example of this in the lives of three women who worked at a salon where both Larry and I go to have our hair cut. The women were godly, but their husbands were not. The burden of their hearts was that their husbands would be saved. Individually, they had prayed for their respective husbands for years. One day, they decided to claim the words of Jesus for themselves: "If two of you agree on earth concerning anything that they ask, it will be done for them by My Father in heaven" (Matt. 18:19). They began to meet together daily before the shop opened to pray for their husbands. And one by one, those men started to open up to God.

During this time, two of the men came to know the Lord; one is now in full-time ministry. The third, who had always vehemently refused to go to church, awoke one Sunday morning and said to the surprise of everyone else in the house, "I think I'll go to church with you today." As long as the wives continued to pray together this way, this man arose and took his family to church each Sunday—unable to believe he was actually there, but nonetheless, there he sat week after week.

Jesus also said, "Where two or three are gathered together in My name, I am there in the midst of them" (Matt. 18:20). It's when two or more are together that the body of Christ can begin to be manifested—the gifts of one given to the others, the prayers of one bolstering and supporting and delivering the others. It takes two or more for the body of Christ to be established. We can't do it by ourselves.

Persevering Prayers

The Lord also calls us to persevering prayers.

We live in an age of instant everything. Many of us don't know how to persevere. If we drive to McDonald's and see too many people in the drive-through lane, we angrily drive fifteen minutes to the next fast-food place—just so we don't have to wait!

Many of us don't know what it means to come again and again and again to the Lord in prayer. Jesus gave us this parable about persistence in prayer:

> There was in a certain city a judge who did not fear God nor regard man. Now there was a widow in that city; and she came to him, saying, "Get justice for me from my adversary." And he would not for a while; but afterward he said within himself, "Though I do not fear God nor regard man, yet because this widow troubles me I will avenge her, lest by her continual coming she weary me" (Luke 18:2-5).

Jesus added, "And shall God not avenge His own elect who cry out day and night to Him, though He bears long with them? I tell you that He will avenge them speedily" (Luke 18:7-8).

Don't be discouraged if God doesn't answer your prayer the first time you pray it. Be persistent!

Our tendency is to do one of two things when we think God is slow to act. One response is to bail out, give up, and walk away. Daniel is a good example to us that we must persist. Daniel fasted and prayed for three full weeks (twenty-one days) before a messenger from the Lord came to him and said, "I have now been sent to you" (Dan. 10:11). He went on to say,

> Do not fear, Daniel, for *from the first day* that you set your heart to understand, and to humble yourself before your God, *your words were heard;* and I have come because of your words. But the prince of the kingdom of Persia withstood me twenty-one days; and behold,

Michael, one of the chief princes, came to help me, for I had been left alone there with the kings of Persia. Now I have come to make you understand what will happen to your people in the latter days (Dan. 10:12–14, emphasis added).

No one knows why some prayers aren't answered immediately. In this case, the angel said that the ruling demon over Persia had intercepted his mission and hindered him from getting Daniel's answer to him any sooner. In fact, the resistance in the heavenlies was so fierce that the angel had to call in Michael, an archangel, as reinforcement. You cannot see the war that is constantly raging in the heavenlies, but one is! You must be persistent in prayer. Don't give up! Just think. What would have happened had Daniel quit praying at the end of *twenty* days instead of persevering all the way to the twenty-first day when the answer from God finally came!

Jesus told His disciples, "Ask, and it will be given to you; seek, and you will find; knock, and it will be opened to you" (Matt. 7:7–8). Those words—*ask, seek,* and *knock*—are all "process" words. They are better translated "ask, and keep on asking," "seek, and keep on seeking," "knock, and keep on knocking." Don't give up! Keep persevering.

If we don't bail out, our other tendency when God seems slow to act is to attempt to take matters into our own hands. Sarah did that by encouraging her husband to have a child by her servant Hagar. That wasn't God's plan, and Sarah suffered, Hagar suffered, Abraham suffered, Ishmael suffered, and the entire Middle East continues to suffer for it today.

Proverbs 14:1 maintains, "The wise woman builds her house, but the foolish pulls it down with her hands." This is true about what we pray, too. Build up your house through prayer. Declare the Scriptures over those you love. But leave the answers to prayer in God's hands, according to His timetable and methods. Don't take those prayers back and attempt to resolve an issue on your own. You may be pulling down your own house!

Tommie Jean is an example of a woman who persevered in prayer year after year for her family. For more than twenty years, she prayed for her husband to be saved and for her children to know the Lord. Through all the years of her husband's alcoholism . . . through the death of her first son . . . through her own bout with cancer . . . through her youngest child's nervous breakdown, Tommie Jean prayed. She told me recently, "All of those trials just made me stronger. As I look back, it seems as if one trial prepared me for the next. I went from strength to strength." The day came, though, when Tommie Jean nearly gave up on her husband. Her son had been healed and had come to know the Lord in a powerful way, and she went to him and said, "I'm going to leave your father. Things have become so bad—I can't go on."

"Wait, Mama," her son said, "I've been studying my Bible and have a promise from God. Matthew 18:19 says that if two of us will agree in prayer, whatever they ask will be done for them by God. You're one, and I'm two. Let's agree every day at noon for Dad's deliverance and salvation."

Things went from bad to worse—the devil's last stand. But then, seemingly from out of nowhere, one day a few months later this man pulled his car to the side of a road, stopped, and cried out to God, "If You can use an old drunk like me, I give my life to You." He was gloriously saved and miraculously delivered from a twenty-year addiction to alcohol in one moment.

That woman of prayer is my mother-in-law; that son, my husband. They did the work of tunneling through the mountain of need in prayer month in and month out. In all, Tommie Jean prayed for the salvation of her husband more than twenty years. But her prayers were answered!

Second Corinthians 4:8-10 speaks to the position of many women I know today who are desperate to see God answer their long-standing prayers:

> We are hard pressed on every side, yet not crushed; we are
> perplexed, but not in despair; persecuted, but not forsaken; struck
> down, but not destroyed—always carrying about in the body the
> dying of the Lord Jesus, that the life of Jesus also may be manifested
> in our body.

You may feel hard-pressed as you pray day in and day out, month in and month out, with no answer. But don't be crushed!

You may wonder what's taking God so long. But don't give up!

You may feel persecuted and abandoned. But take courage in knowing that God has not forsaken you!

You may have setbacks. But as long as there is breath with which to breathe a prayer, you are not defeated!

Revelation 12:11 says that the overcomers who stand in heaven got there because "they overcame him [the devil] by the blood of the Lamb and by the word of their testimony, and they did not love their lives to the death." They persevered, no matter the cost. We, too, are called to persevere in prayer, even, if necessary, to the point of death.

God Needs You!

Are you feeling that nobody needs you today? That nobody cares whether you live or die?

God does!

He needs you to be His representative on this earth.

He needs you to pray so that He can act.

He needs you to be yeast, salt, and light to those around you.

He needs you to be a prophet, priest, and king unto Him upon this earth.

He needs you to raise up righteous seed for the preservation of the Word of God to the next generation and for the extension of His kingdom around the world and to the next generation.

He needs you to nurture and to "mother" the next generation of saints and those who are young in the Lord, to be an example of the believer, and to bind up the wounds of those who are hurting and in need.

God needs you to be a WARRIOR who will not be denied what is yours in God, to fight spiritual battles and win and, thus, to bring about the deliverance of this world from evil!

Yes, you're needed! Desperately so!

15 Desperate to See God Work

"For Yours is the kingdom and the power and the glory forever."

(PART I)

By awesome deeds in righteousness
    You will answer us,
O God of our salvation,
You who are the confidence of all the
    ends of the earth,
And of the far-off seas;
Who established the mountains by His strength,
Being clothed with power;
You who still the noise of the seas,
The noise of their waves,
And the tumult of the peoples.

          —Psalm 65:5–7

What do you do when . . .

You have resisted temptation . . .

You have established a rhythm of life of praying daily the prayer that Jesus gave us . . .

You have declared His kingdom to come on the earth, and that His will alone will be done in your life . . .

You have asked for forgiveness and have chosen freely to forgive . . .

You have faithfully clothed yourself in the armor of God and have built the hedge of protection around yourself . . .

You have resisted fear and have prayed for courage to take on the devil . . .

You have maintained in prayer and agreed in prayer for God's righteous seed to be established on the earth, and you have persevered, doing hand-to-hand combat with the enemy of your soul . . .

In sum, you have prayed with "all prayer and supplication," doing *everything* you know to do . . .

161

And the mountain of need still looms before you as formidable as ever? What *do* you do?

Have you ever found yourself at such a place?

Have you ever prayed so long and fervently for something or some-one that your "pray-er" wore out?

Have you ever reached the point that you are spiritually, mentally, emotionally, and physically exhausted, and yet, the need is still there—but you have no more ability to pray? What do you do?

You must do the only thing you *can* do: stand still and assert, "It is time now, O Lord, for You to work."

That was the position in which Moses found himself as he faced the Red Sea before him and the encampment of Pharaoh's troops just over the horizon behind him.

All had been done that could be done by Moses. He had followed God's instructions and gone back to the court of Pharaoh, entering Pharaoh's chambers again and again to declare, "Let God's people go." He had seen the people of Egypt thrust the Israelites from their presence in the wake of the death angel that had swooped over their land, claiming the firstborn of all children and livestock. The Egyptians had even gone so far as to laden the departing Israelites with precious jewels, money, clothing, and other provisions.

Moses had brought the people this far. And still, they were not delivered. Indeed, they seemed on the brink of destruction. All day, they had heard the distant rumbling of Pharaoh's six hundred chariots drawing ever closer. The people were extremely frightened and cried out to the Lord and to Moses, saying, "Why have you brought us out here to die in the wilderness? It is better to serve the Egyptians than to die here!" The people were in utter despair, more willing to put up with sin and degradation than to believe for a miracle of deliverance and redemption.

In this darkest of hours, Moses stood and gave this word of the Lord to the people:

> Do not be afraid. Stand still, and see the salvation of the LORD, which He will accomplish for you today. For the Egyptians whom you see today, you shall see again no more forever. *The LORD will fight for you,* and you shall hold your peace (Ex. 14:13–14, emphasis added).

When you have done all you know to do in petition before the Lord . . . stand still. Don't make a move. Don't try to bring about a solution in your own strength. Don't try to manipulate the situation. Don't try to force an encounter, a decision, a change. Stand still.

Hold your peace. Be silent. Let your heart be settled in quiet resolve.

And see what God will do. The time has come for trusting the Lord to do your fighting for you.

Burrow into God

A few years ago, during a particularly difficult season in our lives, I found myself at the position where I had prayed for Larry and the ministry until I could pray no more. I had fasted; I had wept; I had prayed with every kind of prayer and supplication I could think of; I had obeyed God as closely as I knew how. Still, the mountain had not moved, and the enemies of doubt, fear, and unbelief stood daily jeering at me. But . . . I was determined to keep standing in faith, knowing with a sure knowing that any help that would come to Larry would come not through flesh and blood but only through the hand of God. Still, the outer, visible circumstances did not look promising; in fact, the situation looked more bleak because there had been no change after such a long time and such intense prayer.

To keep myself in faith and to allow God the opportunity to work, I set myself to dig into God like a chigger. "Dig in like a chigger" is a phrase that we have here in Texas. It means to keep digging in and digging in until you are all the way inside, with nothing visible to the outside world. A chigger is a tiny red insect that will literally eat its way into the body until you cannot see it. I determined to do that in my relationship with the Lord. I dug deep into Him. I hid myself in Him.

I stood and declared, "It is time now, O Lord, for You to work. There's nothing more I can do. There are no more words in my mouth, mind, or spirit to pray. I now stand still and trust You to be our salvation."

When we reach the end of ourselves, we run straight into the sovereignty of God. There comes the time when we need to get our minds off ourselves and our circumstances and place our attention solely on Him.

Yours is . . .

Nothing really matters except "Yours is." All comes from God. All belongs to God. Nothing matters except God and our relationship with Him. All is His.

In focusing on His sovereignty, we set our minds and hearts to survey the majesty of our Messiah, our Savior, the Lord Jesus. Hear the words of the psalmist; voice them aloud:

> You are fairer than the sons of men;
> Grace is poured upon Your lips:
> Therefore God has blessed You
>   forever.
> Gird Your sword upon Your thigh,
>   O Mighty One,
> With Your glory and Your majesty.
> And in Your majesty ride prosperously
> because of truth, humility, and
>   righteousness;
> And Your right hand shall teach You
>   awesome things.
> Your arrows are sharp in the heart of
>   the King's enemies;
> The peoples fall under You.
> Your throne, O God, is forever and ever;
> A scepter of righteousness is the
>   scepter of Your kingdom.
> You love righteousness and hate wickedness;
> Therefore God, Your God, has anointed You
> With the oil of gladness more than
>   Your companions.
> All Your garments are scented with
>   myrrh and aloes and cassia,
> Out of the ivory palaces, by which they have
>   made You glad —(Ps. 45:2-8).

What a Savior we have! What a Deliverer! What a Healer! What a Redeemer! What a Lord!

Rest your eyes. Take them off yourself and your problem or need, and put them on the Lord Jesus Christ. When you come to the end of yourself, you'll discover Him standing there with open arms in full majesty and power.

Speak Courage to Yourself

When you are at the end of your energy to do more and are physically, emotionally, and spiritually exhausted, the time has also come to speak courage to yourself.

I knew this to be true from the early days of our marriage and ministry. Having three babies, all just months apart, and my going one way every morning by bus to school and Larry going the other way to seminary . . . working around the clock . . . doing, going. . . . being wife, mother, pastor's helper, student, daughter, youth choir director . . . I knew the meaning of complete and utter exhaustion. At that point I learned to speak courage to myself. I'd get up in the mornings and look at myself in the mirror and say, "Melva, you can do all things through Christ who strengthens you. The joy of the *Lord* is your strength." And I'd begin to offer up a *sacrifice* of praise.

I'd obey the scriptural command and speak to myself in psalms, hymns, and spiritual songs—singing and making a melody in my heart unto the Lord. Miraculously, I would find *each day* His joy to be my strength. At the end of each day I was still alive and in my right mind! (Well, most of the time!)

Our faith is rekindled daily as we declare anew each morning, "I choose to stand one more day in the strength of the Lord."

In our taking that one small step of faith toward God, God takes one giant step of faith toward us. We act; He enables.

It's a little like getting up in the morning even if you don't feel like it. God doesn't catapult you out of bed in the morning as soon as you open your eyes; it's up to you to swing your legs over the side of the bed. Then He enables you to stand up and walk into your day. That's the walk of faith. You step out in obedience, trusting God, and He enables. Obey and trust. Trust and obey. They are like footsteps moving ever forward in faith.

Are you battle weary today? Have you chosen to stand? To stay standing, encourage yourself in the Lord. Hold on to His promises like a drowning woman desperately clinging to a life preserver! Remind yourself of His promises to sustain you, uphold you, be with you, and stand by you. Remind yourself that He watches over the sparrows, and that you are of more value to Him than they. Remind yourself that He cares for the lilies of the field that last only a day, and that you are destined to be with Him forever. Remind yourself of the words of Jesus: "Lo, I am with you always, even to the end of the age" (Matt. 28:20).

Hold Open the Door

When we stand in faith, having done all we know to do, we are required to do nothing more than hold the door open for God to move on our behalf. We no longer need to wage war or cry out to Him. We trust with all we have that He has heard us and that He is answering, even though we may not see any evidence of His answer. We simply hold the door open for Him, as Ephesians 6:13–14 challenges us: "Having done all, to stand. Stand therefore."

At the same time, we must not hinder or block His moving through that open door. What can hinder the work of the Lord on our behalf? Unbelief.

As a part of our stand in faith, we refuse to entertain doubts or to say to ourselves such things as, "Well, what I prayed must not be God's will" or "I must not have prayed enough" or "I must not have strong enough faith." We must choose instead to die, standing in faith, if that's what it takes. We must declare as Job declared, "Though He slay me, yet will I trust Him" (Job 13:15).

Through the years, I've encountered a number of people who were told that they were terminally ill. Many, even in the face of the most powerful prayers I have ever witnessed, died. We must recognize as we stand in faith that our stance does not guarantee that God will act as we want Him to act, when we want Him to act, or for the reasons we want Him to act. Our stance is what counts for eternity, not His response.

Read Hebrews 11. Again and again you'll read that great men and women of God—men and women who are known for their faith—died without ever seeing that for which they stood believing. Still, their faith counted. God's purposes were accomplished, even if not in their lifetimes. You see, God views things from the perspective of eternity. He alone knows all of His purposes. We see in part; we know in part. For that reason, we stand in faith. We choose to believe. We choose to trust Him for the outcome of His choosing.

Our only position can be that of Shadrach, Meshach, and Abed-Nego who stood before Nebuchadnezzar and proclaimed, "Our God whom we serve is able to deliver us. . . . and He will deliver us . . . But if *not,* let it be known . . . we do not serve your gods, nor will we worship the gold image which you have set up" (Dan. 3:17–18).

You're God's Ally

As I stood in faith this way for Larry and the ministry, the Lord spoke to me and said, "Thank you for being My ally."

Oh, what joy to know that He counts us worthy to be His allies!

When we set ourselves toward God with sure resolve, He encompasses us completely. Can there be any more secure place in the entire creation than to be in the center of God? Right at the heart of His will and purposes! Moving forward in Him! *His allies*.

God would not call us His allies unless He was at work on the problem! We are allies only if we are working together with someone toward the same end. What an encouragement that was to me to know that God was my ally and I was His!

Hear the Word of the Lord to you in your situation today: "We are God's fellow workers; you are God's field, you are God's building" (1 Cor. 3:9). God is working with you as you pray and stand in faith believing. He is bringing about His purposes in your life.

In the assurance that I was and am God's ally, I gained strength. And I learned a fourth great lesson.

God Will Renew You

When we take a position of utter resolve, standing in faith, holding open the door, trusting God daily to act according to His sovereignty, we are renewed.

They who wait upon the Lord *do* have their strength revived. They *do* mount up with wings as eagles. They *are* capable of walking without falling down, of running without becoming weary. (See Isa. 40:31.)

We are told in God's Word that Sarah "received strength to conceive seed" (Heb. 11:11). You will be strengthened, equally so, to bring forth His righteous seed on this earth!

When we stand in faith, the Lord not only acts, but He gives us such an awareness of His presence that we are renewed within.

Are you desperate to see God work today?

Stand back.

Stand still.

Stand courageously.

Stand firm.

And watch!

CHAPTER

16 Desperate to Have More

"For Yours is the kingdom and the power and the glory forever."

(PART II)

Christ in you, the hope of glory.

—Colossians 1:27

For all eternity, all that precedes the Marriage Supper of the Lamb, is preliminary and preparatory. Only thereafter will God's program for the eternal ages begin to unfold. God will not be ready, so to speak, to enter upon His ultimate and supreme enterprise for the ages until the Bride is on the throne with her divine Lover and Lord. Until then, the entire universe under the Son's regulation and control is being manipulated by God for one purpose—to prepare and train the Bride.

—Paul E. Billheimer

I discovered a number of years ago that God's ideal wasn't mine.

I had an image, as all young women no doubt have, of the type of man I wanted to marry. Larry Lea wasn't anything at all like the picture I had in my mind. At the time I met him, he must have weighed all of 135 pounds, and since he was studying so hard—doing four years of college in three—he had deep dark circles under his eyes. He was so intensely focused on God that he seemed to have little time for anything but his studies, prayer, and church services. *Where was my tall, strong, romantic knight in shining armor?*

And yet, I had no doubt—and have never had any doubt—that Larry Lea was and is God's man for me. He is so much MORE than anything I could ever have concocted in my silly girlish mind.

I also discovered that God's ways are not my ways. I ideally would have planned my children to be born several years apart, and instead,

168

we had three babies in three and a half years. I would have chosen to bear our children after I finished my master's degree and Larry finished seminary. That wasn't the way God worked things out in our lives.

And yet, as I stand now with Larry on the brink of a travel schedule that calls for us to be away from home two weeks a month in international meetings, I know that God's timing was unbeatable. Our son is in college; our daughters are nearing the completion of high school. Our children are at an age where we can be away and where they can support us in prayer even as we minister on foreign fields. To have birthed our children at any other time would have been to miss God's timetable for our lives.

I discovered that God's demands on our lives are not always what we find comfortable.

Early in our marriage, Larry went on a mission trip to India and came home with a word from the Lord that we were to sell all of our possessions and give the money to the missionaries ministering to the poor in India. I was not at all enthusiastic about that idea. I couldn't see how being impoverished would be any kind of "good witness" for the Lord. For six months, we—mostly I—struggled with God's call.

Now, it wasn't that we were living in the lap of luxury. Far from it. We had a small apartment, a used car, and furniture that was a combination of "family loan" and thrift shop.

One Sunday I found myself heading for church on my own with our infant son, John Aaron. Larry was ill and stayed home—the only time I ever recall his missing church on a Sunday morning. Alone in our apartment, Larry turned on a television program in which James Robison was preaching. From Larry's perspective, James nearly reached through the television screen to point his finger at Larry as he said, "There's a young preacher listening to me who is not obeying God. Unless you do what God has asked you to do, you'll never be the man of God that God wants you to be." Simultaneously, the Holy Spirit was dealing with me as I sang in the church choir. I knew without any doubt that we needed to do what the Lord had asked us to do in blind faith and obedience. I came home and announced to Larry, "I'm willing to sell all we have and give the money to the missionaries in India." And we did. The next morning we loaded a U-Haul truck with everything we owned and drove away looking for someone to buy our stuff. We sold our possessions to anybody who would give us anything for them, and all the money went to India.

Larry and I know what it means to use public transportation. We know what it is to have a large discarded spool as our dining table and to eat standing around it because there are no chairs. We know what it means to buy our baby's clothes at the secondhand thrift store. We know what it means to sleep on a piece of foam on the bedroom floor—not because that is what *we* chose to do but because that is what the Lord required of us in obedience.

God rewarded us for our obedience. He has blessed us with prosperity we would never have been able to imagine in those early days of marriage. And He also freed us from a love of material things. Today, when God says to us, "Pack up and move," believe me, we're ready to move. We desire to go only where He wants us to go because to be anywhere else is to be in misery.

No, my plan wasn't God's. *His was better!*

I discovered that God's methods weren't mine. I like order, stability, a settled nest. And yet, with three small children to care for, I found myself traveling as an evangelist's wife from city to city in a station wagon packed with diapers and bottles, spending every night in a new motel room. What a tumultuous time that was, and yet one of great joy!

I had learned an important lesson a few months previously that made a great difference in our lives at that time. It was a lesson that probably saved our lives and our family.

One day after I had corrected the children until they were laced so tightly they could hardly breathe, the Holy Spirit spoke to me and said, "Stop it."

"What?" I said in surprise.

He said, "You are grieving My Spirit."

"Me?"

"Yes, you are grieving My Spirit."

"But how, Lord? What did I do? I try so hard to be good, to do everything right."

He said, "Stop trying so hard. Let them have fun."

Fun? The very idea seemed ungodly to me at that time. I was so bent on having everything in order, perfect in all ways, that the thought of fun had never crossed my mind.

The Spirit spoke again, "The fruit of My Spirit is joy. Joy! Let them have some joy."

Instead of hollering, crying, or getting upset whenever the milk was spilled, I chose to laugh. Instead of throwing a fit, I decided to throw a party.

I set out to make life fun for my children—to give them cause for laughter, a feeling of peace, lots of hugs and pats. I set out to make home a place of encouragement for them rather than a place of continual reprimand. And do you know what? My children immediately became healthier. "A merry heart does good, like medicine" (Prov. 17:22)—that's been in the Bible for centuries, and medical science is just now catching up with the relationship between endorphins and the immune system!

And so we set out on the evangelistic trail with JOY in our hearts. It didn't matter that we had no roots. We had one another! It didn't matter that we didn't know where our beds would be that night or that we were living out of suitcases. We had laughter and good conversations and a firm understanding that we were a family.

It wasn't my idea that during my children's middle-school years, God would call my husband to be the dean of a seminary that was located three hundred miles from the church that God also required him to continue to pastor. Common sense would have said to stay in one place and let Larry commute. But that isn't what the Lord planned.

For nearly two years, we lived in one city four days a week and the other city three days. We traveled by plane back and forth, and our children were home schooled. Was it hard? Physically, yes. But through it all, God's purposes were established in our children. At the precise time in their lives when peer pressure could have been so intense, our children became very secure in themselves and in the Lord. Family became their priority over peers. It wasn't my plan. It was God's better way,

God's way is always better than ours.

His power is always greater.

His ideas are always better.

Yours is the kingdom and the power and the glory forever.

When we really face that fact in our lives, we are left with only two things to do: to do all that we can to discern His will for our lives, and to praise Him.

Discern His Will

In discerning God's will, we must begin where Jehoshaphat began—by admitting that we don't have all the answers! King Jehoshaphat awoke one morning to find himself surrounded on all sides by his enemies. There was no way out. Defeat seemed sure.

King Jehoshaphat did what we must do: he "set himself to seek the LORD" (2 Chron. 20:3). He gathered together all the congregation to fast and pray and to seek the Lord. He cried out to God, reminding God of all that He had done for His people and promised to them. And then he proclaimed, "We do not know what to do, but our eyes are upon You" (2 Chron. 20:12). What a powerful statement that is before the Lord!

We truly don't know all that God has in store for us. We cannot see and know with certainty what tomorrow holds. But we can turn to the Lord and say, "I don't know, but my eyes are on You. You know, Lord, and I'm going to follow You wherever You lead and do whatever You call me to do."

In so doing, we are putting ourselves into a position for the Lord to transform our lives and to create us into His bride.

Oh, how important it is for us to catch a glimpse of what it means to be the bride of Christ! We are going to rule and reign with our Lord and Lover someday, as Paul Billheimer so beautifully writes. It is God's purpose that this life prepare us for all that lies ahead. Our real mission—our real identity—comes in eternity.

We will be judging and governing the world and the angels, according to 1 Corinthians 6:2–3. We will have power over the nations, says Revelation 2:26. There's far more to our future than could ever be in our present!

To become the bride of Christ, we must be conformed to the image of Christ. That's what a true bride does. She takes on the name of her husband. She takes on his desires for the establishment of their home and the call of God on their lives. She becomes conformed to what he desires.

Oh, how patient the Lord is as we learn how to be His bride! Larry suffered through rubbery eggs (because I used a rubber spatula to scramble them in the pan), pink underwear (because I didn't know enough to separate the red shirts from the white underwear), and dozens of meals made from Hamburger Helper as I learned how to "conform" to being his wife!

In becoming the bride of Christ, we are not only conformed to His image, however. We are *transformed*.

To be transformed means that we are totally renewed in our minds so that we begin to think like Jesus thinks. We not only do His will; we *desire* to do His will. His heartbeat is our heartbeat. His desires are our desires. We instinctively and intuitively respond to this world as He would respond.

We ask ourselves continually . . .
What would please the Lord?
What would the Lord think of this?
How would the Lord respond?

We act as His Holy Spirit prompts us to act, in accordance with His Word. We live and move and have our being in Him!

To be transformed, we must ever *choose* to seek more of His presence in our lives. We must continually be moving toward Him, weighing all of life's actions and decisions against His will and purposes.

Praise Him!

Nothing transforms us as much as praise!

To see God at work, to know God's will, to experience God's deliverance, to enjoy God's protection, and to taste God's provision is to praise Him! To praise Him is to see Him work, to know His will, and to experience His power.

Just as our lives begin and end in Him, so must our prayer. "Yours, O Lord," we declare, "IS the kingdom and the power and the glory forever. You alone are worthy to be praised. You alone know the beginning from the end of our lives. You alone have the power to sustain us. You alone are the Most High!"

As Tim Hansel tells us, praise is always a choice. We choose to begin to praise God *in* our circumstances, regardless of what they are. Why? Because God is God, no matter what. Because God alone can change things. And because praise is the language of faith.

Praise looks at the mountain before us and says, "God is greater!"

Praise keeps all that you have prayed activated. As you walk away from your time of daily prayer, praising God and declaring that all comes from Him and belongs to Him, sin and doubt and unbelief are given no toehold. It's impossible to commit sin when you are truly praising God! It's impossible to be tempted when you are in the act of worship! It's impossible to doubt God when you are extolling His praises with all your being! Praise focuses your mind and heart solely on the Lord and creates an atmosphere around your life wherein God can release His angelic host to do its work, acting on your behalf and executing vengeance against the enemy of your soul.

Even when you don't feel like praise, choose to praise. Make your praise a "sacrifice" of praise. It may not be easy, but that's not really the point. He is *worthy*!

Praise is the one thing that you will be doing forever. It is the language of heaven. It is the song of the angels. Why will you be praising the Lord throughout eternity? Because the Lord will *forever* be worthy of your praise.

Praise Transforms Us

Much of our prayer focuses on our needs—our need for identity in Christ, our need for forgiveness, safety, and provision. Praise focuses on the Lord and His identity. In turning outward, we actually bring renewal inward. To continually focus on oneself is self-destructive. In fact, it's a sign of mental sickness! To focus outward on the Most High God is to forget self and at the same time put ourselves into the position for God to integrate us into the "self" that He wants us to be.

Praise is meant to be unwavering. May we say as the psalmist did, "My heart is steadfast, O God, my heart is steadfast; I will sing and give praise" (Ps. 57:7). And as we offer a sacrifice of unwavering praise, we are filled with greater resolve, fortitude, and strength inside. We become His unwavering witnesses.

Praise is meant to be continual. As we praise God "for all things" and "always" (Eph. 5:20), we are filled with His continual presence.

Praise is meant to be extravagant. We can never praise the Lord beyond what He is worthy to be praised. Our most lavish outpourings of love can never exceed His worthiness to be loved. And yet, the more we praise the extravagance of the Lord, the more we become aware of His abundant giving into our lives—of peace overflowing, of ideas overpowering, of power overcoming, of love overwhelming, of blessing to the point that there is not room enough to contain it.

Praise is meant to be unceasing. As our hearts turn toward the Lord all day, we are aware of His presence filling us all day.

Everything we praise the Lord FOR, He becomes TO us and IN us!

And the more we praise Him, the more we become like Him.

The Desire to Have More

We live in a world that craves "more." We want more for our money, more activities to cram into our time, more time for our activities, more love, more health, more of everything!

The more we look to the acquisition of external, outside things to satisfy that craving, the more we are disappointed.

That is never true about the Lord. The more we crave Him, the more we are satisfied within and without,

Are you desperate today to have more?

Choose to be desperate to have more of the Lord!

Choose to be transformed into His likeness.

Choose to lose your identity in Him.

You'll find that you gain not only His identity but your own.

God will establish His kingdom through you. He will reveal His power through you. He will show forth His glory through you. He will cause you to be all that you can be and more than you ever imagined.

The more desperate you become to have more of Him, the more delighted He is to pour Himself into you.

I received a letter recently in which a dear saint of God wrote,

Dear Melva,

I've been praying the Lord's Prayer for six and a half years, and I'm more desperate now than ever, part of the reason being that the more intimate I have become with Jesus, the more I have had to face my own inadequacies and inabilities. But since I began praying through the Lord's Prayer with the Holy Spirit, desperation drives me to Jesus, where before it drove me to sin.

In Christ,
Gay

Through the desperate times of *your* life, let desperation be the tool of God to drive you TO Jesus, not away from Him. Make your desperation serve God. Let it work for your good, conforming you to the image of Jesus.

Yes, be desperate . . .

To have more of Him!